WITH THE RED DEVILS AT ARNHEM

Personal Experiences with the 1st Polish Parachute Brigade 1944

Marek Święcicki

Translated from the Polish by H.C. Stevens
Additional material and footnotes added by Niall Cherry

Helion & Company

Helion & Company Limited
Unit 8 Amherst Business Centre
Budbrooke Road
Warwick
CV34 5WE
England
Tel. 01926 499619
Email: info@helion.co.uk
Website: www.helion.co.uk
X (formerly Twitter): @Helionbooks
Facebook: @HelionBooks
Visit our blog at https://helionbooks.wordpress.com/

Published by Helion & Company 2013, new edition 2024
Originally published by MaxLove Publishing Co. Ltd. 1945

Designed and typeset by Farr out Publications, Wokingham, Berkshire
Cover designed by Paul Hewitt, Battlefield Design (www.battlefield-design.co.uk)
Illustrations © as individually credited

ISBN 978-1-804516-57-7

British Library Cataloguing-in-Publication Data.
A catalogue record for this book is available from the British Library.

For details of other military history titles published by Helion & Company Limited, contact the above address, or visit our website: http://www.helion.co.uk

We always welcome receiving book proposals from prospective authors.

Contents

List of illustrations

The original captions are printed in italics. More detailed captions have been provided, where applicable, by Niall Cherry.

List of maps

List of abbreviations

A.F.P.U.	Army Film & Photographic Unit
C.O.	Commanding Officer
C.R.E.	Commander Royal Engineers
C.W.G.C.	Commonwealth War Graves Commission
D.S.O.	Distinguished Service Order
DZ	Drop Zone
G.P.R.	Glider Pilot Regiment
G.S.O.	General Staff Officer
K.O.S.B.	King's Own Scottish Borderers
L.A.D.	Light Aid Detachment
L.Z.	Landing Zone
O.C.	Officer Commanding
P.P.B.	Polish Parachute Brigade
R.A.P.	Regimental Aid Post
R.E.	Royal Engineers
R.E.M.E.	Royal Electrical & Mechanical Engineers
R.M.O.	Regimental Medical Officer

Introduction to new edition by Niall Cherry

Poland had a chequered history, up until the formation of the 'Second Polish Republic' in the aftermath of the Great War following the break-up of the Austrian-Hungarian Empire. The country had a brief existence amid deteriorating relations between Germany and the rest of Europe. In 1939 it became the target for further German expansion and on her eastern border lay the USSR and its leader Stalin, who also had designs on occupying Poland. On 1st September 1939 German troops crossed the Polish border, and within days Britain and France had declared war on Germany and given Hitler three days to withdraw his troops from Poland. This was ignored and later, on 17th September, as part of a secret deal between Russia and Germany, the Red Army also entered Poland. Within a few days Poland was occupied, and would not be an independent state for another 50 years or so. Leading Polish figures managed to escape and a Polish Government-in-Exile was formed in Paris. An embryonic Free Polish Army was created in France, but within months was forced to flee again, this time to England. Among those who escaped to England was Colonel Stanislaw Sosabowski. In September 1941 it was decided to form a parachute unit made up of Polish volunteers. Colonel Sosabowski was selected to command this unit, which was to be an 'independent brigade group' containing infantry, medical, artillery, transport and engineers at least.

During the early part of its life, command of the brigade was retained by the Polish Government-in-Exile, with the promise that it would drop into Poland as soon as conditions were right to assist with an uprising. In 1941, however, this seemed a distant dream. As time went on, the British realised that a drop into Poland would be totally impracticable and they wanted to use the brigade to take part in the campaign in France after the June 1944 invasion. The commander of all the British airborne troops in England, Lieutenant-General F. Browning, who had been involved with the equipping and training of the Poles, had offered Sosabowski command of an airborne division if he would allow the Polish Parachute Brigade (P.P.B.) to be under British command. Sosabowski resisted the offer, stressing the Poles' desire to remain true to their original role. Political pressure was brought down on the Polish Government and they agreed to allow the P.P.B. to carry out one operation after the invasion and then be allowed to go to Poland.

As a result, in June 1944, the P.P.B. moved from their barracks in Scotland to the Stamford and Peterborough areas in Lincolnshire, as part of the 1st Allied Airborne Army. In August 1944 they were placed under the command of 1st Airborne Division and warned they would be required to take part in forthcoming operations. Sosabowski, by now a Major-General (due to the Polish system of promotion – based on service and ability irrespective of the position held), was an outspoken critic of some of the operations planned, especially Comet. Additionally the Poles had few friends in high places and no representation at 1st Allied Airborne Army H.Q. and it was this formation that would decide the P.P.B.'s immediate future. The Brigade was not particularly strong, numbering about 1,700 compared to over 2,000 in a British parachute brigade, and morale was not helped when, during a training exercise in July, two Dakotas collided over Tinwell, near Stamford, and killed 26 members of the Brigade.

I should like to thank several people who helped me with the additional information contained here. In no particular order except alphabetically, they are Luuk Buist, Steve Elsey, Geert Maassen, Robert Sigmond and Robert Voskuil.

Niall Cherry was born in London in 1959 and recalls becoming interested in military history as a schoolboy from watching such classic war films as *The Battle of Britain* and *A Bridge Too Far*. He later found out that one of his grandfathers fought in the Great War, serving as a chemical corporal at Loos in 1915, and ending his career as a Captain. His father served in the REME in the 1950s and Niall continued in the family tradition by serving in the RAMC. During his time he qualified as a Combat Medical Technician Class 1 and as an instructor in First Aid and Nuclear, Biological and Chemical Warfare, and ended as a Senior NCO.

Deeply interested in the major conflicts of the 20th Century he has visited numerous battlefields, including the Western Front, Arnhem, Gallipoli, Normandy and North Africa. He is a long-standing member of the Western Front Association, the Military Heraldry Society and 23 Parachute Field Ambulance Old Comrades Association. He also has the honour to be the UK representative for the Society of Friends of the Airborne Museum Oosterbeek and secretary and a trustee of the Arnhem 1944 Fellowship.

He has now written seven books – *Red Berets and Red Crosses, I Shall Not Find His Equal, Most Unfavourable Ground, With Nothing Bigger than a Bren Gun, Striking*

Back, *Tunisian Tales* and *Arnhem Surgeon*. He has led various groups around battlefields, contributed articles to *After the Battle* and *Battlefields Review* and has assisted with around 30 books on the airborne forces and the Great War.

Niall currently lives in Lancashire and works for BAE Systems in the aerospace industry.

Introduction

This book contains a graphic description of the very gallant part played in the battle at Arnhem by the 1st Polish Parachute Brigade Group.

The name of this Brigade will always be linked with that of the 1st British Airborne Division in connection with this action.

R.E. Urquhart, Maj-.Gen.
17th November, 1944.

Foreword

The battle of Arnhem is too recent to be susceptible of detailed analysis and expert criticism. It occurred only a few weeks ago, and all that can be said of it at present from the strictly military aspect is that this operation of the First Allied Air Army constituted the greatest airborne offensive yet seen in this war. The force fighting at Arnhem was the spear point aimed at the vital arteries of the German Army in Holland, and, recognising its danger to all their plans for defence, the Germans fought desperately to eliminate the threat.

The object of the airborne landings in Central Holland was to secure bridgeheads for the British Second Army advancing from the south, so overcoming the problem of fighting for every river crossing, of the Maas, the Waal, and the Lek (the lower Rhine) not to mention the many canals which intersect Holland. The length of the wedge, from the initial starting point of the Second Army to Arnhem was some eighty miles. Arnhem, the point of the wedge, was the scene of the most exposed and remote landing of all, and the forces dropped there knew that they were fighting against tremendous odds.

The following pages, describing scenes of the battle around Arnhem, have been written by Marek Swięcicki, a Polish war correspondent who was attached to the Polish Parachute Brigade. Part of the brigade was landed by gliders on September 18th, the second day of the operation, on the northern bank of the Lek, close to Arnhem.[1] Accompanying this group, he was an eye-witness of the fight put up by the British Airborne Division and the Polish Parachute Brigade during the following seven days. He was present at the landings made by the Polish brigade later in the week, and shared all the anxieties, and uncertainties of the crucial days when the brigade was scheduled to seize the crossing of the Lek and link up with the British Division. Until that was achieved only part of the brigade, taken across to Holland in gliders, and suffering heavy losses, had been able to fight at the side of their British comrades.

Owing to weather conditions in England it was impossible for the rest of the brigade to land in Holland until September 21st. By then the enemy had had

1 The glider element of the Polish Parachute Brigade actually landed on Monday 18th and Tuesday 19th September 1944, the second and third days of Operation Market Garden. There were 10 gliders landing on the second day and 15 on the third.

time to mass his infantry and artillery to deal with the landing, and the British Division had been driven back on to the heights west of Arnhem and away from the river bridge. The Polish Brigade landed on the south bank, east of Driel, and had to fight its way to the ferry crossing at Oosterbeek. But by the time it reached the crossing the Germans had succeeded in destroying the ferry and bringing the river under continual fire. Consequently, at dawn of September 22nd the section of the brigade on the south bank found that it could not hope to make the crossing in daylight, and had to hold its ground against furious German attacks until nightfall. Only by night were the remnants of the brigade able to cross by improvised ferries, and despite the vigilance of the German observation posts.

By this time it was obvious that unless aid came from the Second Army, moving up from the south, the Airborne Division could not hope to hold its positions on the north bank. For three more days the Division fought, living in that hope of the break through from the south. At one time the guns of the Second Army came into action, and the men of the Division raised their heads to hear British shells flying over them into the German positions. But even artillery was not enough to keep the situation from deteriorating tanks and infantry failed to get through to the river bank in sufficient strength to achieve permanent contact with the force on the Arnhem side.

During the night of September 25th-26th the British Division with the remnants of the Polish Brigade withdrew from the northern bank of the Lek, under cover of the artillery fire of the Second Army, and through the bridgehead held on the southern bank mainly by sections of the Polish Parachute Brigade.

The story Marek Swięcicki has to tell is not history, but a living narrative of what he, an eyewitness, saw and experienced during those tremendous and glorious days of the battle for Arnhem. As such they form a tribute to the gallantry and heroism of the men—British, American and Polish—who dared all in that desperate adventure, and through whose determination to hold on and hold out the drive to Arnhem as over 80 per cent successful. Eighty per cent? Only now, as the Germans are being swept right out of Western Holland, as the British, Polish, Canadian and American troops are reaching the bank of the Maas in their northward drive, and now that at any time they will have crossed the Waal and moved on to the Lek, does one begin to realise all the importance of that stand at Arnhem which enabled the Second Army to advance beyond the river Waal and so prepared the way for the final ejection of the Germans from Holland.

The "Red Devils" will, many of them, yet contribute greatly to the final victory. But they and their Polish comrades in arms will have no finer story to tell than that of Arnhem, to which this book is devoted.[2]

Ryszard Kara-Malaszkiewicz,
Chief of Staff, 1st Polish Parachute Brigade

2 To assist the reader in understanding the composition of the P.P.B. the following may help:

In September 1944, like the rest of the 1st Airborne Division, the P.P.B. was based in the East Midlands and consisted of the following units. The list includes commanders and the approximate number of men who took part in the operation:

- Brigade HQ (Major-General S. Sosabowski) based at Stamford, 104 men plus 9 British liaison officers.
- 1st Battalion (Major M. Tonn) based at Easton-on-the Hill, 354 men.
- 2nd Battalion (Major W. Ploszewski) based at Wansford, 351 men.
- 3rd Battalion (Captain W. Sobocinski) based at Peterborough, 374 men.
- Anti-Tank Battery (Captain J. Wardzala) based at Blatherwycke, 132 men.
- Engineer Company (Captain P. Budziszewski) based at Wansford, 133 men.
- Signals Company (Captain J. Burzawa) based at Easton-on-the Hill, 93 men.
- Medical Company (Lieutenant J. Mozdzierz) based at Stamford and Blatherwycke, 93 men.
- Seaborne Echelon (Captain A. Siudzinski who originally travelled with the 1st Airborne Division's sea-tail), 43 men.
- Light Artillery Battery (Major J. Bielecki), only 5 junior officers and 1 liaison officer went by air with the 1st Airborne Division.

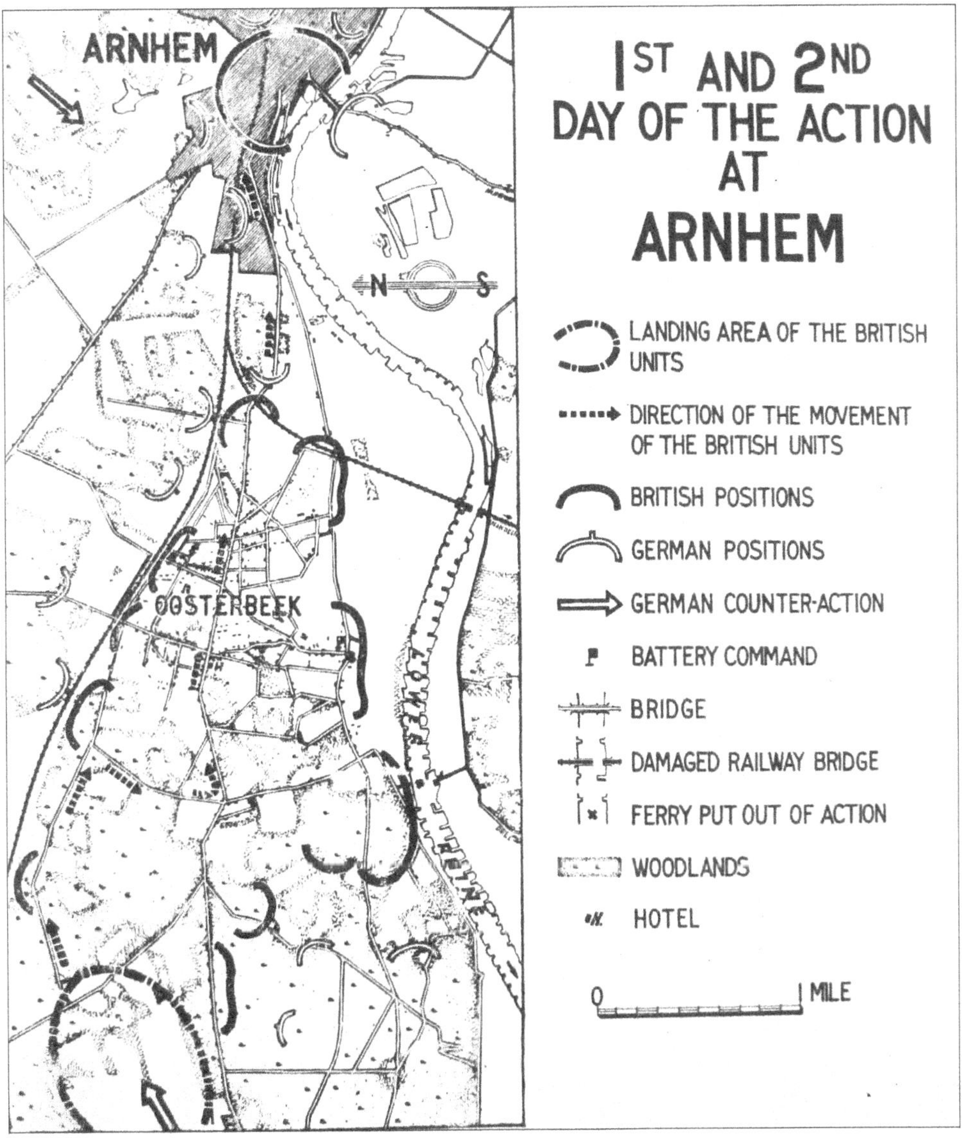

First and second day of the action at Arnhem

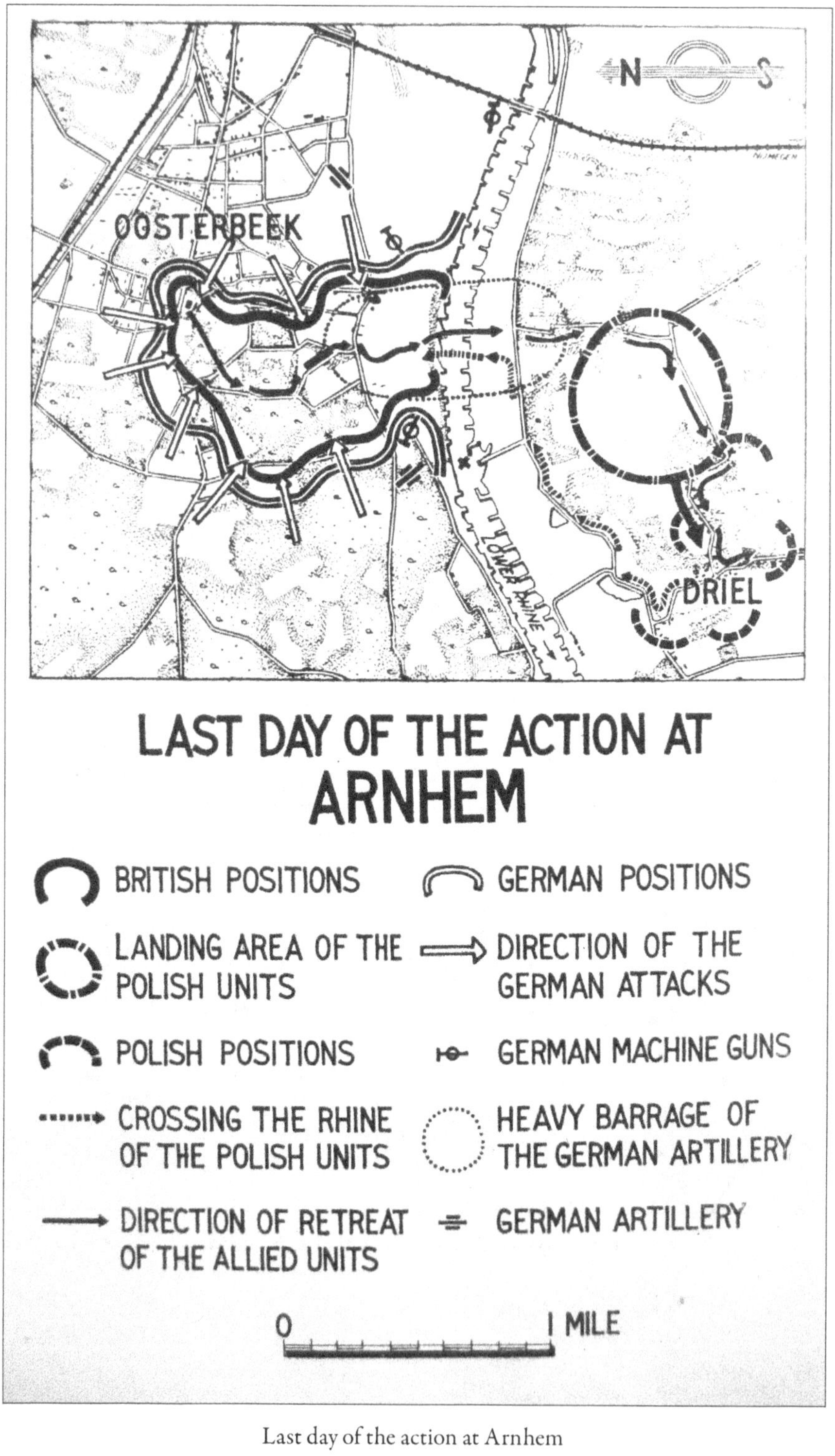

Last day of the action at Arnhem

The End of Waiting

"So tomorrow I'm taking the first lift of the Airborne Division to Holland," remarked Squadron Leader Robert Jamieson,[1] a tall, broad shouldered New Zealander. "Jamie" was interested in everything: in European politics, European coins and stamps, the brands of whisky and beer, but at this moment perhaps he was most interested in the geography of Holland.

"It may be a stiff job," glider-pilot Lieutenant Maclean,[2] a good looking Scot with large blue eyes muttered meditatively.

"But a fine opportunity for a war correspondent. You'll get some good stories," Jamie remarked to me, then, addressing himself to nobody in particular, he asked the quite unnecessary question: "Who says another drink?"

He was answered with a contemptuous silence. As if there could be any doubt about it at such a moment! Of course, we'd have another drink!

We were in the small, very crowded bar of an R.A.F. station "somewhere in Southern England."[3] It was the evening of September 16th, 1944. The landing of the First Allied Air Army in Holland had been decided upon. The first landing group would be flying tomorrow, the second the following day, and further parties on successive days.

We all remarked to one another: "At last!" Those two words dominated our feelings and were the best expression of our spirit. For almost six weeks we had been waiting in the cold, muddy transit camps for this operation. We dragged ourselves out of one tent and into another, we travelled from station to station, we studied the orders, plans and maps of new operations almost every day. But

---

1 Squadron Leader R. Jamieson was a member of 296 Squadron based at R.A.F. Manston in Kent and flew Albemarle aircraft. He took part in the first lift flying P1432 carrying either members of the 2nd South Staffords, 181 Airlanding Field Ambulance, the 1st Airlanding Anti-Tank Battery or, somewhat uniquely for a British crew, towing a Waco glider carrying U.S. air support signal parties.

2 This 'Lieutenant Maclean' is a bit of an enigma. Perhaps as the book was being prepared in 1944, he wanted his name kept secret, because as far as is known there was no officer with this name in the 1st Airborne Division. There was a Lieutenant Maclaine of Lochbuie who it is believed was a section commander in 14 Flight of F Squadron, who on the morning of 17th September 1944 took off from R.A.F. Blakehill Farm in Gloucestershire. There is a photo taken at R.A.F. Broadwell, close to Blakehill Farm, showing him with other officers on that morning. In any case both stations are a long way from R.A.F. Manston in Kent. A possible explanation is that it was Lieutenant Mackee, an attached British liaison officer.

3 Meaning R.A.F. Manston near Ramsgate in Kent.

Our final cup of tea with the Y.M.C.A.

The scene at Saltby aerodrome on Thursday 21st September 1944 as men of the P.P.B. wait for the fog to clear so they can fly to Holland.

the Western Front steadily advanced.[4] What yesterday was a serious assumption,

4 This table may give the reader an idea of how many operations Marek may have been briefed for.

Between June and September the 1st Airborne Division (or, for some operations, just a part of it) were warned of quite a number of different operations. Even today there is controversy about exactly how many operations there were. I will just list the operations stated in the book by Lieutenant Colonel T. Otway, *Airborne Forces, Second World War 1939-45, Army*' (London Imperial War Museum 1990 reprint), who was asked to compile the official account of the British Airborne Forces in the Second World War. Issued in 1951 it remained a 'restricted document' until it was reprinted by the Imperial War Museum in 1990, and to which interested readers are directed to obtain details of the following operations. Note: some were planned (and cancelled) so quickly they never received an official name.

1. Operation Tuxedo
2. Operation Wastage
3. Reinforcement of the U.S. 82 Airborne Division 7th to 10th June 1944
4. Operation Wild Oats
5. Operation Beneficiary
6. Operation Swordhilt
7. Operation Hands-Up
8. Operation Transfigure
9. Operation Boxer
10. Operation Axehead
11. Operation Linnet
12. Operation Linnet 2
13. Operation Infatuate
14. Operation Comet
15. Operation Market-Garden

And now the take-off.

The men boarding a Dakota of 32 Squadron of the 314 Troop Carrier Group at Saltby. I would assume that the man wearing a beret near the door is a medic with his white armband. Numbers 32 and 50 Squadrons, both flying from Saltby, took a mixed bag of units from the P.P.B. to Arnhem, including men from the Brigade HQ, 3rd Battalion, Engineer Company, Medical Company, Transport and Supply Company, Signal Company and the Anti-Tank Battery.

today became an illusion, and tomorrow might prove to be nonsense. We were being out-stripped by the armoured divisions, which more and more robbed us of hope of going into action and being of some service. "We'll have to go to Burma," Lieutenant Tom Baron[5] of the Airborne Division Artillery Regiment had declared a week before. "There's no work left for us in Europe."

While Lieutenant John Widdicombe,[6] sadly shaking his head, added:

"I always did incline to think the Continent is rather an incalculable factor."

Now Tom Baron and John Widdicombe were to take part in tomorrow's operation. Not to Burma, but to Holland. Despite the many capricious turns of fate, the Continent was not going to make a mock of bur hopes.

"All the best!" we raised our glasses.

"Good luck! Time, gentlemen; time!" The barman wished us success, and

5 Lieutenant T. Baron was actually Lieutenant T. Barron, who was Gun Position Officer of A Troop of the 1st Airlanding Light Battery of the 1st Airlanding Light Regiment Royal Artillery.

6 Lieutenant J. Widdicombe was Assistant Command Post Officer of the 3rd Airlanding Light Battery of the 1st Airlanding Light Regiment Royal Artillery.

then pointed meaningly to the clock.

We bought some more cigarettes. As many as we could get, for there might not be any, "over there." Then we went to bed.

As next morning I watched the dozens of Stirlings starting with the Horsa gliders in tow, I knew for certain that this time the operation would not be called off. That I would not be going on to another transit camp. That I would not be turning up in London for a few hours' leave and have shamefacedly to explain why I was still in England. Our war had begun ... [7]

"A good start!" Jamie said in the mess, on his return from taking over the first group to Holland. "The flak was very poor. So far as I could judge the gliders landed without difficulty. All our ships returned to base."

"Fine!" we rejoiced. "We ought to do as well." And, filled with optimism, we went off to tea.

7 As far as is known no Stirlings towing gliders took off from R.A.F. Manston on 17th September 1944. It is thought that 56 gliders took off from Manson on this day, all towed by Albemarles from 296 and 297 Squadrons. These were 46 Albemarle/Horsa combinations and 10 Albemarle/Waco combinations.

As stated before these took South Staffords, gunners, medics and American signal parties to three landing zones Z, S and N. Z and S were in the vicinity of Wolfheze, whilst N was near Nijmegen.

Names which brought success

We had painted three names on the nose of our glider, Irena, Krystyna, and Barbara. They were the names of three Polish girls; two of them were in England, and one in Rumania. We were sure that these three names would bring us luck. At the moment of our departure they were the expression of our hope and faith in the success of our operation. They were also the unfailing tribute which even the most phlegmatic of men pays to sentimentality at a critical moment.

Johnny Cotterill[1], the first pilot of our glider, looked at those three feminine names with understanding and sympathy, but Max Hunter[2], the second pilot, had a definitely ironical expression on his face. Johnny was a youngster with a thin and very immature moustache. Max was a little older and posed as a cynic. They both declared that they were very glad to be piloting a glider full of Poles.

"It's a little more unusual!" Max said to justify his satisfaction.

"Have some?" Johnny offered us some chewing gum. "You may need it."

A large Y.M.C.A. canteen car distributed tea. Two American sergeants with film cameras in their hands ran about the aerodrome and took miles of film. They took a special fancy to our glider, and filmed us in front of it and inside it, in our berets and without them, in our overalls, with our lifebelts and in every other conceivable way. Someone gave us the days' papers. I got the *Daily Herald*; right across the front page was a banner headline: "Allied Air Army Invades Holland." I read a long communiqué on yesterday's landing, superficial descriptions of preparations to date, and then a long article on Generals Brereton[3] and Browning

---

1 5109253 S/Sergeant J. Cotterill G.P.R., believed to be of 3 Flight of B Squadron, he returned across the Rhine at the end of the battle.

2 14281802 Sergeant J. Hunter G.P.R., again believed to be of 3 Flight B Squadron, he was killed on 25th September 1944 aged 28 and was one of the 57 men first buried in the garden of the Ter Horst house by the Old Church in Oosterbeek. He now lies in the Arnhem Oosterbeek War Cemetery grave 3A20. The 10 gliders flying from Manston that day contained the following loads for the P.P.B.:

- 7 Horsas carrying No 3 Troop of the Anti-Tank Battery with five 6 pounder anti-tank guns, men, jeeps, trailers and associated stores.
- 2 Horsas carrying the 'heavy equipment' of the Engineer Company.
- 1 Horsa with the advance party of the P.P.B. H.Q.

All of these gilders landed safely on LZ X at Renkum.

3 Lieutenant-General L. Brereton was in command of the 1st Allied Airborne Army which had been created in August 1944 to co-ordinate the activities of the various British and American airborne units in England and of the air transport units required to take them into action. Until being given this job,

and the appeal of the Dutch Government in England to the people of Holland.

"So they know already in London! That's fine!" I said with satisfaction, as though the fact that my friends in London had learnt of our operation could in anyway influence its course.

At last we were ordered to embark. The doors were slammed, the steps removed, our glider was hitched on to a tractor, which hauled us off to the runway.

The weather was heavy and cloudy, and large drops of rain ran down the sides of the glider. We were surrounded by a grey, impenetrable gloom. At the moment of starting we could not even see the ground, the English ground which during the years of war and enforced exile had become almost as dear to us as our own soil. We were a little moved, and to rid ourselves of the feeling we turned once more to studying the maps and plans of the operation.

We had no consciousness whatever of movement, we could not feel that we were flying. The density of the air at first prevented all bumps and tugs; there was no sudden drop or sudden rise.

The glider made its first sudden drop at the same moment as the first rays of the sun broke through. Now we were over the Channel, England was behind us and the mist was behind us. A broad ray of sunlight broke through to us, then a second and third and many more. It suddenly grew light, the glider wallowed more and more from side to side and reminded us of a roundabout in a travelling fair.

The sight which the sun revealed to us was an imposing one. We seemed to be flying along a long, endless avenue, amid very many Stirlings and Horsas. Captain M.,[4] an artillery officer by profession and mathematician for the love of it, went to the pilots' cabin with the ambitious intention of calculating how many there were. He counted more than once, beginning first from the right side, then from the left, but without result. Although all this force of the Air Army was flying in perfect order, the outlines of machines and gliders blended with one another, into a single mass, like telegraph poles seen from the window of an express train.

"Well, this is going to be an operation!" Captain Zwolanski[5] rubbed his hands with satisfaction.

But, leaning across from his seat, Johnny Cotterill said with a note of anxiety

---

Brereton had been commander of the US 9th Air Force. He based his H.Q. at Sunninghill Park near Ascot and his British deputy commander was Lieutenant-General F. Browning.

4 It is thought that Captain M. is Captain A. Mackowiak, who was a gunner. His job at Arnhem appears to have been 'liaison officer' to the British artillery.

5 Captain L. Zwolanski was GSO3 (Intelligence) at the H.Q. P.P.B. but attached to 1st Airborne Division H.Q.

in his voice:

"Will there be room enough for us to land?"

Above the coast of Holland we were greeted by the fire of anti-aircraft artillery. But it was quite weak, apparently completely harmless, and seemed rather like a salute of guns. We laughed contemptuously, removed our rubber lifebelts, put on our overalls and drank the tea we had brought with us from the aerodrome. Later still we smoked our last cigarette before landing and fastened ourselves firmly to our seats, as the pilots ordered us.

Below us were forests, and canals glistening in the sun. We could see hardly any roads and not much trace of human being, of human communities. Nor large groups of houses, hardly any traffic on the roads. After the juicy green of the English landscape, the green of the Continent, of Holland, seemed a little grey, as though covered with dust, or rather withered. The forests looked larger than those of England, and the broad, irregular stretches of land along the coast and the canals were also larger. And, of course, there were windmills. So many of them that we could not but notice and remember them even from the height at which we were flying.

When we cast off from our Stirling a growingly deep and intense silence enveloped us. For a couple of seconds, accustomed as we had grown to the penetrating roar of engines, we were a little surprised and benumbed. But the former roar was very soon replaced by a new, much softer sound, of quite a different kind. It was the sound of machine-gun and rifle fire coming up to us from the ground. Not too friendly a welcome for us. It reminded us yet again that we had taken on a great adventure.

The glider violently, brutally touched down and rolled over the earth in little bounds, to stop at last suddenly. We broke open the doors, jumped out and fell just as all the regulations, instructions and exercises had taught us to – to the ground. The soldiers released the safety catches of their weapons, and we set up a Bren gun, trained on the forest. Shots were coming from the forest, more and more thickly. The enemy was not more than two hundred yards from us. But now troop-carriers roared out of the Hamilcars landing beside us and drove off to pacify the forest. A glider not far from us caught fire and flamed swiftly, like a match. Men jumped out through the thick smoke.

"All okay!" they shouted.

They could look after themselves. Another glider fell right up by the line of forest. Their situation would be worse. . . . We must get out of this open field as quickly as possible, for Messerschmitts might come flying over. They were our

A patrol in kilts on the way to Arnhem.

It is believed this photo shows the C.O. of No 1 Wing of the Glider Pilot Regiment, Lieutenant Colonel I. Murray, discussing a move towards Arnhem. This photo was taken on the morning of 18th September 1944 by Sergeant D. Smith of the A.F.P.U. attached to 1st Airborne Division. Smith noted the title as 'jeep patrol setting out to go into Arnhem.' It was on the Utrechtseweg in western Oosterbeek opposite the junction with Bredeweg. The kilted officer on the right is Captain J. Ogilvie, second in command of D Squadron of the G.P.R. and the officer on the right is believed to be Lieutenant K. Strathern, the Intelligence Officer of D Squadron. James Ogilvie is believed to have drowned while trying to swim the Rhine on the night of 25th/26th September 1944; his body was recovered on 17th October 1944 and is now buried in the General Cemetery C.W.G.C. at Rhenen. Today the Bredeweg is called the Kasteelweg.

quiet but continual, persistent fear. Where the devil was the German air force, anyway? We had expected it to be waiting for us over the sea, or, at the least, over the coast of Holland. But although we hadn't met it yet and. although it wasn't yet over our heads, that did not justify us in tempting Providence. We climbed into a jeep dragged out of the glider, and drove rapidly away from the landing point.

The weather had turned perfectly fine. It was three in the afternoon, and the sun was as hot as though it were mid-summer. We made our way along a romantic and pot-holed road through a forest. The road greatly reminded us of the Continent, and most of all of Poland. And the forest, too, was like the Polish

The woods around Arnhem are full of surprise.

It is believed this photo was taken somewhere between Driel and Elst.

forest. I pointed this out to Max, but he was thinking his own thoughts, and had his own dreams:

"Why d'you think it's like Poland?" he asked in surprise. "This road and forest remind me of South Wales, they're the same colour, even."

We passed a group of houses scattered about in front of the forest. The people brought water and milk out to us on the road. Children gave us apples.

A young girl brought armchairs, chairs, settees and carpet out of one house. She set them all out in the sun and dusted them. Some domestic rite, we supposed.

"There's to be a wedding in that house tomorrow," an old grey-headed Dutchman informed us in perfect English. And then, as though he had suddenly remembered something, he added: We welcome you with all our heart to our country. We've been waiting for you a long time, but at last you've arrived."[6]

6 It is thought this café is the Hotel van Dijk on the main road (Wolfhezerweg) leading south from the village towards the Utrechtseweg just by the railway station. Today it is a restaurant called De Tijd.

My First Dispatch

"Hallo, boys!" I gave a friendly shout to a dozen or so British soldiers sprawling in cane chairs on the verandah of a wayside café on the main road to Arnhem. The soldiers awoke and stared at us with scowling faces.

"Shut up!" a corporal snarled.

"Let them be!" a captain, standing to one side, in a torn and dusty overall said in a conciliatory tone. "We've all had a hard night; we've been in action for almost twenty-four hours. . . ."

"Sorry!" I muttered in embarrassment, and withdrew to my jeep.

We drove on by a road through dense trees, which united above us in an entanglement of boughs and leaves, forming a roof or vaulting. The afternoon sun was declining and through this vaulting cast a twilight of a peculiar colour and mood on the road. It was a twilight half melancholy and half solemn. But it at once turned sombre when we saw our first dead German by the roadside. The lad, a big fellow enough, had fallen outstretched along the green of the roadside, and now blended with it by the colour of his uniform. His tin hat had fallen off his head, and his mouth was stretched in an odd, rather macabre smile.

"One!" Max counted ferociously, to add: "Two ... Three ... " as he caught sight of more German bodies.

But he suddenly ceased counting, for a British soldier was lying by the road. All these men, exhibiting their bodies and their death to public view, seemed amazingly shameless. And there was something inexpressibly tragic in the traces of struggle along this truly beautiful and now very quiet road. We were filled with a feeling of embarrassment, caused both by the war which we had brought here and by our very presence, which because of those soldiers on the café verandah seemed to be belated, unnecessary and smelling of a cheap and vulgar triumph after their efforts, their heavy, twenty-four hour struggle.

But we had no time for reflection. A cross roads presented us with a picture amazing even in war, original even in such circumstances as ours. In front of us was an elegant German military car; riddled through and through, like a sieve, with Bren gun bullets, and the men who had not succeeded in escaping from it. Half hanging out of the car were two figures. One of them was wearing the uniform of a German general. Two narrow streaks of blood had congealed on his gold epaulettes. His trouser selvedges were red, too, but his long black boots shone irreproachably. His right hand, in a white leather glove, gripped a revolver; in his left was an unfinished cigarette. The general had a youthful, handsome face, and a severe profile, his hair was combed up, he had very dark eyes, which at that moment gazed calmly up into the blue scrap of sky between the green crowns. I bent over him and read his name on the small tablet hanging from his neck: Major-General Kussin. [1]

The driver lay on the other side of the car, his face downward. In the back seat, in attitudes which suggested that they had tried to hide behind each other, in mortal terror of the bullets, two German non-commissioned officers were frozen for ever in an extravagant embrace.

We found the command of the Airborne Division about a mile beyond the crossroads, in a fine, large and pleasant hotel at Hartenstein. The hotel was situated by the road-side and was surrounded by a park which opened straight into an extensive forest.[2]

On the road were large numbers of jeeps. Jeeps were also drawing up and driving off from the hotel building. Among the trees soldiers were digging the first anti-aircraft and slit trenches. I was amazed at these precautions, for the memory of our triumphal journey was still fresh in mind.

"What are the trenches for if we're going on farther tomorrow?" I asked thoughtlessly.

"All sorts of things happen in war," Captain M. answered circumspectly. "Hope for the best, prepare for the worst," as the English say.

1 Generalmajor F. Kussin, Field Commander 642 (Arnhem District), had been visiting the commander of SS Panzer Grenadier Depot and Reserve Battalion 16, Sturmbannführer Krafft, at the Hotel Wolfheze in that village on the afternoon of the 17th and had been advised not to use the main Utrechtseweg to get back to his HQ in Arnhem, but ignored this advice. When he turned onto the Utrechtseweg from the Wolfhezerweg he ran into 5 Platoon from B Company of the 3rd Parachute Battalion and his vehicle was shot up. He and the two other passengers, Unteroffizier M. Koster (batman/interpreter) and Gefreiter J. Willeke (driver) were killed. They remained in and around the bullet-riddled Citroen car until Tuesday 19th September when Padre Pare (No 1 Wing G.P.R.) assisted by two German POWs buried all three at the side of the road. One of the A.F.P.U. men, Sergeant D. Smith, took several shots of the car and bodies. Later the three Germans were moved to the German war cemetery at Ysselsteyn in southern Holland.

2 In the original plans for Market-Garden the H.Q. of the 1st Airborne Division was going to be at a pre-war Dutch Army barracks called 'Artillerie Park' in grid square 7378 in north-west Arnhem. They obviously never made it here and I suspect the Hartenstein Hotel was looked on as a temporary H.Q. pending a move closer to Arnhem. This building reverted to a hotel after the war and is now the Airborne Museum.

The first person I met as I jumped out of the jeep was smiling Major Roy Oliver, Chief of the Public Relations Service. Behind him was the tall and thin figure of Alan Wood of the *Daily Express*. There were also Flight Lieutenant Williams and B.B.C. correspondents, Stanley Maxted and Guy Byam.[3]

"When will you be bringing your first despatch?" our press dictator asked solicitously, measuring me with a rather reproving glance from behind his large spectacles. It seemed that the major was saying: "So much to write about, you've been in this country two hours and still nothing ... You can't go on like that!"

"I shall be coming to see you today, Major," I said, and asked how things were going.

"According to plan," Major Oliver answered, while Alan Wood nodded his head, in its overlarge tin hat, which slipped about with every movement he made.

The main doors to the hotel were blocked with rifle butts. The floor of the hall was covered with glass, plaster had fallen from the ceiling, the floor was littered with papers and carpets collected from all over the building. Overturned chairs emphasised the military and aggressive atmosphere of the place. Amid the rubbish a sergeant major from the Divisional Staff stood with an irreproachable smile on his face. Despite his appearance, at that moment he reminded me of the smiling and courteous manager of some fashionable London hotel.

"There are rooms still vacant upstairs, sir," he said to me. "The ground floor

3 There were a number of members of the press and 'war correspondents' accompanying the 1st Airborne Division on the various lifts; in nominal charge of them was Major R. Oliver, the 'Army Public Relations Officer'. He was assisted by two censors, Captain P Brett and Flight Lieutenant B Williams. So as well as the three A.F.P.U. men, six reporters went to Arnhem, Alan Wood of the *Daily Express*, Jack Smyth of Reuters, Stanley Maxted and Guy Byam of the B.B.C., Major Tony Cotterell of the War Office's pamphlet *War* and Marek Święcicki for the Polish press. Tony Cotterell accompanied the 1st Parachute Brigade to the road bridge and was taken prisoner there and subsequently killed in a battlefield atrocity at Brummen on 23rd September 1944. On this day a group of mainly officer prisoners was being taken to Germany in an open lorry when several made an escape attempt by jumping out of the vehicle near Brummen post office. One of the guards supposedly panicked and turned his weapon on those in the back of the lorry. Four men were killed instantly with two more later dying of their wounds. These six were:

- Lieutenant T. McNabb 1st Airborne Reconnaissance Squadron
- Private G. McCracken 2nd Parachute Battalion
- L/Corporal S. Allen 2nd Parachute Battalion
- Captain H. Platt 1st Airborne Reconnaissance Squadron
- Lieutenant S. Mills D Squadron Glider Pilot Regiment
- Major A. Cotterell

All six are now buried in the Eastern General Cemetery at Enschede Holland.

Major-General R.E. Urquhart, C.B., D.S.O., commander of the 1st British Airborne Division.

This photo was taken on Urquhart's return to England on Friday 29th September in the personal C-47 of General Williams of IX Troop Carrier Command, which flew him from Brussels to R.A.F. Cranwell in Lincolnshire. He was met here by General Brereton and a series of photographs were taken by a US Army Signal Corps photographer called Tonne. 4 glider pilots also came back on this aircraft - S/Sergeants J. Bonome and H. Cawnter and Sergeants D. Hartley and J. Woodward.

is entirely occupied as offices."

I wandered from room to room, and everywhere found traces of our predecessors. Everything looked as though the people who had been living here had only just left the house. And that was true, for they had gone hence only very recently. We had met one of them, General Kussin, barely fifteen minutes ago.

The room I finally decided to occupy had a fine view on to the forest and many newspapers on the table. Beside them were writing paper and addressed envelopes: to Hanover, Kiel, Berlin. With women's names: Frau, or Fraulein. One post-card began with the words: "My dear Martha," went on to tell the writer's love and yearning, and ended "Heil Hitler."

"I've found a couple of bottles of wine," Max shouted, arriving unexpectedly. "Johnny's getting supper ready."

At the end of the corridor was a large room in which were our two captains,

Major-General Stanislav Sosabowski, commander of the Polish Paratroop Brigade.

Bruce Davis,[4] a glider pilot of the American air force, who had been brought down somewhere on the road by German artillery and had a wound in the leg, also Maclean and Johnny. They were discussing our situation, which seemed very good. Our forces were already in the suburbs of Arnhem. One of our battalions was in the very centre of the town, but was temporarily cut off from the main forces. The enemy strength in Arnhem couldn't be very great, surely not more than two thousand men.

"We'll be in the town tomorrow, that's sure!" Bruce Davis declared[4].

Maclean also thought so, and I too. Only Captain M. shook his head

4 This Captain B. Davis was in fact not a glider pilot but an American Air Force officer who had ended up at Arnhem almost by mistake. In mid-August the newly-formed 1st Allied Airborne Army became concerned that some of the operations being planned well behind the German lines would have no protection against German air raids. The R.A.F. did however, have mobile radar stations which had operated with ground troops in numerous theatres of operation, with the intention of calling up friendly fighters to intercept any intended raids. So two R.A.F. units with equipment capable of being carried by Horsa gliders were formed. These were 6080 and 6341 Light Warning Units. It was planned to send two in the hope that at least one would reach the area. The use of these R.A.F. units at Arnhem is a sad story which space does not permit to be told here, but each of the two teams contained an American fighter control officer. However, on being told that no U.S. fighters would be operating in the Arnhem area, they were told they could withdraw from the operation. One chose to do so but the other, Lieutenant Davis, volunteered to stay with the R.A.F. unit and was one of the thirteen Americans who went to the Arnhem area with the 1st Airborne Division.

doubtfully.

"The Germans are defending the town and that's their great chance. Only flame throwers and armour or heavy artillery and mortar fire could clear them out quickly and effectively. And we haven't got any."

I found the same anxiety late that evening in the staff. They were satisfied with the two successful landings, of yesterday and today, but they were not excessively optimistic. The German resistance in Arnhem was particularly desperate. They were fighting with a savage fanaticism. The capture of Arnhem would be a difficult task.

But during the night exceptionally good news came in: in a storming attack our forces had captured the bridge in the suburb of Arnhem.[5]

"Attacks were made one after another. It was impossible to reach the approach to the bridge: the Germans put down a curtain of fire from mortars and. machine-guns. Our losses were growing heavier and heavier, and time was passing," someone told us in the dark corridor. "We had failed to take the Germans by surprise at the bridge. So we had to think of something that would make up for the lack of the element of surprise. Something which at one blow would change the intolerable situation. Our commander decided to send in jeeps and Bren guns to take the bridge."

"How many jeeps took part?" I asked.

"Fifteen set out. Only ten managed to establish a bridge-head on the other side. That original form of attack cost us five jeeps. But men, most of all. . . ."

I ran upstairs and began my first despatch to London, writing by the light of a torch:

"September 18th. Monday. Holland. The German command in Northern Holland was taken completely by surprise by the landing of the Allied Air Army. Thanks to our air supremacy the airborne troops arrived without losses at the landing place. The Germans are fighting desperately."

5 As Marek's story is dealing with the Monday, this comment about the bridge being captured uses a bit of 'journalistic licence.' Some of the 2nd Parachute Battalion (and a few others) reached the road bridge in the late evening of the Sunday, having covered the eight miles or so from their dropping and landing zones. Having first secured the northern end of the bridge they made a couple of unsuccessful attempts to take the southern end. By the Monday morning, whilst they held a small perimeter around the northern end, efforts by the rest of the Brigade to reach them were unsuccessful. In fact a small book could be written on the fighting in western Arnhem and the attempts to reach the bridge area. One of these attempts was a suggestion to form a 'flying wedge' of the few Bren gun carriers present in western Arnhem together with jeeps loaded with ammunition to try and force their way to the bridge. But this was cancelled when it became clear that the German opposition was too strong and it would be a suicide mission.

An International P.O.W. Camp

On Tuesday, September 19th, I was awakened by the sun which was flooding all my room. All was quiet outside, and that in fact disturbed me most of all. Had the Division gone on? No, the Division had not moved at all, only everything around the hotel looked different. On the quiet road of yesterday anti-tank guns were standing. In the forest the troops were digging in, dozens of tenches showed yellow with their ramparts and green with the camouflage of tree branches. There was definitely less jeep traffic; they were parked under the trees, and all the most necessary articles reserves of ammunition and 24-hour food rations, had been taken out of them.

There was hardly any fresh news of the struggle. In fact the situation had changed very little since yesterday. The Germans were bringing up reserves and evidently intended to surround us. But our reserves would also arrive: in the afternoon the Polish Parachute Brigade would land on the southern bank of the Lek. Approximately in the same place as we had landed, the glider force of the Brigade would be landing today. The Brigade would come into action immediately, to form the second half of the pincers around the German defence. And then the end of the entire campaign would follow: Arnhem occupied, the bridge over the Lek captured and held by our forces, contact between the forces on the Lek in the neighbourhood of Arnhem with the forces on the Waal in the neighbourhood of Nijmegen would be made. It was to be expected that the first two days would be especially critical. But now those two days were past. Undoubtedly the operation would develop successfully.[1]

In general, the staff opinion confirmed my own expectations. In this situation the best talk I could have would be, of course, one with General Urquhart, but he was not to be caught. He had driven off to our forward positions and was there studying the development of the Division's attack. But the intelligence officers proposed a different idea to me:

"We've already got lots of prisoners. There are Poles among them, too.

1 As Marek states, on this Tuesday the P.P.B. was due to land on DZ K, which was about one mile due south of the road bridge. A second instalment of their heavy equipment was due to come by glider and land on LZ L, which was north of the river. The P.P.B. were at Saltby and Spanhoe airfields ready to take off but both places were covered by fog which curtailed any flying that day. Perhaps this was a fortunate intervention by the weather, as the area around DZ K was in German hands.

Wouldn't you like to talk to them?"

Of course, I would. For that matter, everything seemed to be in a state of suspense at the moment, so I could not see anything else to do.

The prisoners of war camp was situated on a tennis court, a couple of hundred yards from the hotel. The prisoners had removed their uniforms and were sunbathing. The netting around the court had nothing in common with the unpleasant associations of the barbed wire which usually surrounds prisoners' camps. And the German soldiers also looked carefree. They stared at us curiously, when we entered this improvised transit camp, and one private asked me right out whether we had brought any cigarettes with us.[2]

"We've got enough food, for we're getting your 24-hour rations, but the cigarette situation is not so good," he explained.

The prisoners were a mixed lot, in ages, nationalities and types of arms. Some of them were only fifteen or eighteen years old, and there were Germans, Dutch, Russian and Poles. Infantry and artillery, remnants of panzer forces and S.S. men. Perhaps S.S. men most of all. There were no older men among the S.S.; in every glance, in the behaviour, in every movement and even in the bearing f this picked Hitler guard we observed obstinacy, determination and hatred.

"The S.S. men are the worst," said the intelligence officer in charge of the camp. "They refuse to give any personal details and I can't convince them otherwise. These whelps have been told that we kill prisoners. 'You'll shoot us all the same,' they said, pale with fear, 'so why should we answer your questions?' They're tremendously surprised when they get food instead of the bullet they expect. But their surprise very quickly gives place to arrogance and sheer rudeness."

The Poles were sitting in a separate corner of the camp. They were drawn from Poland's western areas, which Germany had incorporated illegally with her territory, and had then illegally conscripted them into the German armed forces.

"I come from Silesia, from Katowice," one of them told me. "Two years ago I was summoned to the local office and told I had got to go into the army. I

2 The tennis courts at the rear of the Hartenstein were used as a P.O.W. cage by men of the 1st Airborne Provost Company assisted by glider pilots. One of the more famous Arnhem photos taken by Sergeant D. Smith on 18th September shows four S.S. prisoners, of which one in the group was only 17. Yet the other three appear to be tough and even in captivity show an air of arrogance. Joe Kitchener, one of the glider pilots in the shot, commented to me when questioned about them that he didn't think they were inexperienced troops and were a mean tough group.

answered that I was a Pole, and also that I was 42. 'As you're a Pole and you're 42 we'll send you and your family to the concentration camp at Oswiecim,'[3] the official shouted at me. And I know what Oswiecim meant. I was frightened not for myself, but for my wife and children. The boy's fourteen and the girl eleven. How could I sentence them to death?"

Another Pole, who also was in his forties, had been doing forced labour in a factory in Western Germany. When the Germans began to form "volunteer" detachments from the workers, he was taken by force, given a uniform, and sent to France.

"And couldn't you run away?" I asked.

"How could I? We were always watched, and we were never allowed to be together. There were several of us in the company, but we were distributed into different platoons and sections."

They asked avidly for news from the West. By every word and sentence they uttered they expressed their certainty that Germany would lose the war, that she was bound to lose it. They had believed that for five years. Only it had been difficult to hold out at times. And it had been difficult to find an answer to the German propaganda.

"Only when the Allies began to bomb our district, yard by yard," said the man who had been working in Germany, "did we feel that the general smashing of the Germans had begun. Our foreman, a Nazi and sadist, at once grew less truculent, and whenever he got drunk he shouted that now surely the Germans were "kaput."

"And our major shot himself during the retreat," another Polish prisoner intervened in the talk. "We were quartered in the Limoges district, and when the Allies broke through the Normandy front we fled without stopping day and night through France and the whole of Belgium. We ran short of petrol, so we had to march on foot, we threw away our baggage and. weapons, and only when we reached Holland did the Germans set to work to reorganise new forces from our remnants."

Close by Russians, Ukrainians, Georgians, Kirghiz, Cossacks were lying. There was one Mongol and two Tartars. They eagerly stretched out their hands for cigarettes, but otherwise were quite apathetic.

"What will you do now?" I asked one of them.

He shrugged his shoulders and had no answer to make. They knew only

3 In German the town of Oswiecim became known as Auschwitz, the infamous extermination camp in Poland.

that there was no return to Russia for them.

"The Red Army regulations lay it down that a soldier of the Revolution is not taken prisoner. If he is, he ceases to be a Soviet citizen," a sturdy, swarthy Ukrainian informed me. He looked to be an educated man, and the leader of the entire group. Before the war he had been a teacher, all his family was in Russia. Of course, he would like to go back, but if it wasn't possible ... He smiled bitterly and asked for another cigarette.

"Will they put us into the army in England, too?" a Cossack with the letters S.S. on his uniform collar asked circumspectly.

I shook my head doubtfully.

The camp also contained Dutchmen who had joined the German forces in Holland. Among them was a little, ugly woman, about forty years old, the secretary of the Arnhem Gestapo.

"We owe to her very many death sentences and still more imprisonments in concentration camps," said one of the Dutch patriots who accompanied us during this inspection. "Rarely has the word 'Quisling' had a worse connotation than in her case."

Another woman prisoner was a young and ugly blonde belonging to the German Auxiliary Air Service. She had just returned from leave to Arnhem when she had this unpleasant surprise of the Allied air invasion.[4]

The German "Waaf" smiled at us uncertainly as we passed and very timidly said: "*Gut Morgen*."

4 This member of the German Auxiliary Air Service was Irene Reimann, who was the only female German prisoner of Arnhem. She was a telephone operator at the Diogenes H.Q. bunker of the Luftwaffe 3. Jagd-Division at Schaarsbergen and billeted at Wolfheze. She had been apparently out for a Sunday afternoon stroll with her German boyfriend when she was taken prisoner in the Buunderkamp woods by men of B Company of the 7th K.O.S.B. She appeared in a cine film taken by Sergeant G. Walker of the A.F.P.U. on this day. She was later moved to the P.O.W. cage at the Hartenstein, where on Wednesday 20th September she was photographed by Sergeant M. Lewis being given a cigarette by one of her glider pilot guards, S/Sergeant J. Price of E Squadron.

Between Fire from Heaven and Earth

About one o'clock Dakotas flew over and dropped supplies for us. The German artillery at once concentrated all its fire against the sky. The fire was considerable in quantity but, fortunately, not very effective. Successions of shells burst in the area around the large, slowly circling machines. The pilots decided to drop their supplies exactly on the spot indicated on their maps. It was a difficult task, for we were not holding a large area. In addition, at no great distance all around us were German guns. Without doubt more than one pilot was already faced with the problem, on that third day of the Arnhem battle, of how to drop supplies to ensure that they fell into the right hands.

Precision has to be paid for. Suddenly one of the machines, which had flown too precisely into the area, caught fire with a brilliant red flame. Then two more. In terms of percentages the losses were not very high, but we could not think in terms of percentages. We were depressed, and Corporal Douglas expressed our feelings when he said:

"They're real heroes!"

Truly, to circle continually amid that violent fire called for very strong nerves.

Yet the sight was beautiful and colourful. The dark grey Dakotas against the pale blue sky, the black clouds of bursting shells, hundreds of red, blue, yellow, green, violet and white parachutes with supplies provided a broad scale of colours and made one admire modern warfare, despite its foul menace.

Two or three machines dropped their packages right down to us, by the hotel and in the surrounding trees. They crashed through the branches, and the first windows broke with a jangle of glass. This crashing and jangling seemed very loud, and the enemy's artillery was deafening. That blessed day we did not yet know that all this was only an anaemic prologue, that our war was really only just beginning.

The sun was just as hot as yesterday and the afternoon was just as quiet as, on low rises beside the railway track, we awaited the arrival of the Polish gliders.

In front of us the Red Devils had taken up positions covering the landing site.[1] There was no one in the field. The forest on the horizon was perfectly quiet. Some distance of, on the farther side of the track, mortars were whistling. We could not decide which way the mortar shells were flying, but it was certain that they were not coming our way. It seemed that they were firing into the Arnhem suburb, against the first British Brigade, which was attacking. The minutes and the quarters passed, but the aeroplanes did not come over. We were beginning to ask ourselves anxiously what this meant, when at last tiny dots in the sky began to draw near, growing and growing, until at last we could see that they were Stirlings and Horsas. Over the landing ground the Horsas grew still larger and closer. Cast off from the tugs, they would be landing in a moment.

But at that very moment something happened which we had not expected. From the north other tiny dots, much more nimble, grew and grew, racing up to overtake the sluggish Horsas. Messerschmitts! Their machine-guns snapped and barked. It grew hot and terrible in the air. Several gliders caught fire and, rolling over from wing to wing, dived in a mad flight to the ground. Several others landed helplessly with shattered undercarriages. Even from some distance we could see the torn walls and hanging rudders. One of the gliders broke up in the air like a child's toy, and a jeep, an anti-tank gun and people flew out of it. We had never expected things to be so bad, so very bad.

The Polish soldiers who succeeded in escaping the Messerschmitts' fire and managed to land swiftly poured out and unloaded their gliders. The Messerschmitts circled for some time over the landing ground, raining machine-gun bullets down on it. When they stopped the forest opened up. Skirmishing Germans, looking in the distance like rabbits jumping, or field mice, moved rapidly and inexorably forward, striking at the numerically much weaker British guards, throwing them back and forcing them to withdraw. The

1 The area chosen for the P.P.B. second lift of equipment was LZ L, which was located to the north east of the village of Wolfheze and north of the railway line that ran almost east to west across the landscape. This was the third glider lift for the 1st Airborne Division and as well as some waifs and strays from the first and second lifts, consisted of 15 Horsas flying from R.A.F. Keevil carrying men and equipment from the H.Q., Signals, Medical and Transport and Supply Companies. The total cargo carried was 22 jeeps, 11 trailers and 35 men. They were towed by aircraft from 196 and 299 Squadrons and the glider pilots came from a variety of squadrons including A, B, D and E.

An additional 20 Horsas allocated to the P.P.B. flew from R.A.F. Tarrant Rushton; these were towed by aircraft from 298 and 644 Squadrons. The loads consisted of 20 jeeps, 10 trailers, 10 6-pounder anti-tank guns, 16 motorcycles and 74 men, all from the Polish Anti-Tank Battery. The gliders were again piloted by a mixture of men from (at least) A, C and G Squadrons. Of these 35 gliders it is believed 28 made it to LZ L.

landing ground was already in German hands. The German infantry fired at the gliders which had escaped the Messerschmitts and had not caught fire.[2] The bullets tore through the gliders' wooden walls, over the jeeps and guns which had been brought out, and then over the men, throwing more and more of them to the ground.

The men who had escaped whole fled. Yes, they fled; for it couldn't be called a retreat or a defence. They were stupefied by the fury and strength of the attack, which was for them, the new arrivals, and for us, a complete surprise. About a mile from the landing-place I came across the few wounded men who had succeeded in escaping from the massacre. Lieutenant Wróblewski tried to smile at us from his jeep, though both his legs were shattered and ribs were broken.[3] Beside him lay a corporal with two bullets in his chest. But there were only a few wounded or whole. The majority, the great majority, had remained on the landing ground, or were taken prisoner. And only a few guns reached Hartenstein. These guns went straight into position, reinforcing the British anti-tank defence. A few days later they effectively held attacks of German 'Tiger' tanks.

After the optimistic mood of yesterday, we now experienced hours full of gloomy presentiments. The German defence had put its fangs out, and, unfortunately, they were powerful fangs.

In this situation the German air force was the most unpleasant surprise of all. So there was a "Luftwaffe" after all, we must reckon with that fact!

In the evening more gloomy news: the Germans had recaptured the bridge our jeeps had captured yesterday.

The black-out regulations were tightened up in the hotel at Hartenstein. It was forbidden to shine any light outside or even to smoke cigarettes. The light was turned off in all the main part of the building. The inhabitants of the

---

2 In spite of the best efforts of 7th K.O.S.B., who had been positioned around the LZ as local defence, the Germans were able to fire on the landing gliders. To make matters worse the 4th Parachute Brigade, which had been fighting in the woods to the north and north east of LZ L, had received orders to disengage and make for Wolfheze. As they started to move across the LZ and were pursued by German troops, the gliders started to land and unload. As one might imagine, it became a chaotic situation, with troops firing on each other and the Germans. It is believed only three of the ten anti-tank guns were unloaded; one of them was commandeered by an officer believed to be from the 10th Parachute Battalion and never seen again. Two of them made it to Oosterbeek under the command of 2nd Lieutenant W. Mleczko. Also flown over was Major-General Sosabowski's personal jeep – this was unloaded safely but on the drive to Oosterbeek was intercepted by the Germans and the driver wounded and captured. When the Germans found a suitcase with Sosabowski's name on it, they broadcast that he was dead.

3 2nd Lieutenant A. Wróblewski was 2 i/c of No 1 Platoon of the Anti-Tank Battery, P.P.B.

first and second floors evacuated to the corridor of the ground floor, or sought places in the trenches.

The war was beginning to look much less pleasant than we could have expected only a few hours before.

The Concert Begins

The parachute group of the Polish Brigade did not arrive on Tuesday.

"But they might come today?" we asked one another on Wednesday morning.[1]

For a change the day was cloudy and cold. We could hear the enemy fire coming closer, but it still did not arouse any great anxiety. Several men, duty, tired, unshaven, arrived from the advanced posts of the First and Fourth Brigades. A hard struggle was going on in the sectors held by these brigades. The Germans had received reinforcements, and had fresh forces at their disposition. Our men were tired; they were fighting without rest and were suffering heavy losses.

I was standing by the road with a group of Poles when mortars began to whistle. This was the first time they had been so close and so heavy in their fire. Branches cracked and fell with a loud rustle to the ground. Several shouts arose. We flung ourselves down on the ground by the road one alongside another, to take up as little surface area as possible. That apparently is of some use. I was next to Lieutenant Halpert,[2] one of the Polish officers who had escaped from yesterday's massacre of gliders.

"Get up, the war's over," I said to him when everything was quiet again.

"You're right, so far as I'm concerned the war's really over," he said with a mournful smile, pointing to his left leg. It was peppered with shrapnel. A crimson patch of blood was widening over the ground.

But medical orderlies were already running up. There were other wounded around us. The mortars had caught men around the jeeps, on the road and along the tracks, on the hotel verandah, everywhere. We still possessed the psychology of conquerors; we still did not feel like taking to trenches.

"That was a good lesson," Lieutenant Futer, from the Divisional

---

1 As we have seen, the P.P.B. should have arrived on D+2, which was the Tuesday, but on this fourth day once again the weather in England intervened and stopped any aircraft taking off. Perhaps the only good bit of news was that a message had got to England from the 1st Airborne Division that the original DZ K south of Arnhem road bridge was not viable and suggested that the P.P.B. be dropped further west around the village of Driel and use the ferry located nearby to cross the river.

2 Lieutenant J. Halpert was commander of the 2nd Platoon of the Anti-Tank Battery.

Headquarters, remarked.[3]

I had crawled along to his trench for a minute or two. With him were Johnny Gotterill, Max Hunter, and two or three other glider pilots, and we all set to work to persuade one another that a trench is the most comfortable place to spend one's life in.

"We'll have the bedroom here, and the dining room there," Max gave rein to his imagination, pointing to the two opposite ends of the trench.

And to demonstrate that there really was reason for a dining room he took a packet of biscuits out of his pocket. Lieutenant Futer added a piece of chocolate and some chewing gum. We hadn't reached starvation point yet, so I made a face and said that I'd have some tea. For it is quite easy to make tea on the special stoves with which we had been provided.

"You're mad," the Englishmen grew indignant. "Who ever drinks tea at twelve o'clock?"

To which I had no answer except to take umbrage. In my by no means perfect English I uttered a remark or two bitterly about conservatism, and was on the point of jumping out of the trench when up they started again! Shell after shell. They were still dropping them in our area. So I settled down humbly on the bottom of the trench and muttered

"Sorry! I don't want any tea."

They roared with laughter.

An hour later we climbed out to go and meet the Polish Brigade. There were several of us Poles: three liaison officers, a liaison patrol from the field transmitting station, and myself. It was quiet again now, and men were climbing out of the trenches. We passed along our detachments, and then across the positions of the Airlanding Brigade. We entered a part of the forest not yet brought within active military operations. The broad, smooth road seemed far from war. People's faces stared out through the windowpanes of the few houses we met with.[4]

"Is anything serious going to happen here?" a stout Dutch woman asked me, from her doorway.

3 I have been unable to trace any officer at Arnhem with the name of Futer; my guess is perhaps Marek meant Lieutenant R. Falck. He was O.C. of No 4 Section of the 1st Airborne Provost Company and his section was responsible for security duties, escorts and the prisoner of war cage. So he was highly likely to have been around the Hartenstein.

4 DZ K was now near Driel and so this group headed almost due south from the Hartenstein and ended up in the Light Regiment artillery line around the Old Church in southern Oosterbeek – an ideal spot to see if the P.P.B. did arrive.

"Of course not, we're here," I unthinkingly answered.

We crossed one of the main roads leading to Arnhem. We passed tramlines, and came into Oosterbeek, a large village which was almost a suburb of Arnhem town. Through gardens and around buildings we approached the positions held by our artillery. The men were quietly eating lunch and making tea. We were stopped by men holding one of the houses, and they treated us to part of their rations.

"Everything's going better," a little corporal with ginger moustaches said. "And when your brigade arrives everything will be fine. Bacon or bully, sir?"

"I always did say that you're better off in the line than at staff headquarters," one of our staff officers muttered half to himself. "We've hardly got anything to eat, and here they're feeding like fighting-cocks."

A little farther on, in another small wooden house we found the command of one of the batteries. The command was organised in the cellar. They hospitably invited us downstairs, but we preferred the fresh air. The wireless operators were setting up their station, discussing questions of waves and frequencies, when …

Yes, mortars again. Into the complete silence and peace suddenly tore an avalanche of fire and noise. Not far away boards, beams, and rubble went flying into the air. I heard the crash of trees and the jangling of breaking glass. I was standing just outside the house door, and, as though given a violent push, or perhaps moving instinctively, I fell through the doorway and groped down the ladder into the cellar. Others behind me. Outside, the shells went whistling overhead.

We couldn't understand what was happening. Where had these mortars come from? It was only a couple of hours ago that they'd been firing at the Divisional Command. Now they were firing here. Well, that meant the Germans were attacking us from both ends of our positions. In other words, we were surrounded. That was a logical deduction, yet it seemed so incredible by comparison with our recent situation that I found it difficult to believe. I asked the British officers what they thought.

"It must be so," they answered.

I asked the Polish officers.

"It seems like it," they said.

Then what would happen to the Polish Brigade? For it was to help the Division in its attack, it was to be the final blow, the last nail in the coffin of the German defenders of Arnhem. What would it do now that we were

Polish Signal Men in action.

British troops dug-in on the western edge of the perimeter with wireless operator in foreground.

This photograph was taken by Sergeant D. Smith on 21st September in a garden of a house in the Van Lennepweg in Oosterbeek. It shows men of H.Q. Company of the 1st Borders defending the western side of the Oosterbeek perimeter.

All around Hartenstein Hotel.

This photograph was taken on 24th September by Sergeant D. Smith, and was actually the last one taken by the A.F.P.U. men at Arnhem. It shows the Divisional Admin Area behind the Hartenstein. This area had been an easy target for the German artillery and mortars. On the previous Thursday a fire had broken out in the dump which was only extinguished with great difficulty and on Friday the Germans caused two fires and a stack of 6-pounder shells exploded due to a direct hit. Fires were also caused on the Saturday. The A.F.P.U. team had gone with enough film to last two days but managed to eek it out for eight. Apparently Sergeant M. Lewis was saving a roll of captured AGFA colour film to shoot the arrival of the 2nd Army. Apart from this their stocks had been exhausted.

surrounded, and the Germans were on the opposite, southern bank of the Lek, too?

But at that moment the telephone rang. They were ringing from the Divisional Command to say that the Polish Brigade would not be arriving yet. Not until the afternoon, at the earliest.[5]

For the moment at least my anxieties were a little premature.

5 The P.P.B. arrived at Saltby and Spanhoe about 0845 in the morning, to be told of the change of DZ, about 4 miles to the west of the old one. At 1000 the men were told that the arrival time at the DZ was being moved back 3 hours. At about 1340 engines burst into life and the Dakotas started to taxi down the runways. However, this was as far as they got this day. The fog and drizzle that was covering England was, according to the weather men, even worse on the route to Holland, with thick cloud going up to 9,000 feet. The drop was called off for that day.

Awaiting the enemy.

Another shot taken by Sergeant D. Smith in the Borders area, this time on 24th September. It shows on the left Major W. Neill, OC C Company and Lieutenant J. McCartney, the OC of 28 Medium Machine Platoon.

We left the cellar and saw that everything all around looked very different from what it had half an hour before. The little coach-house, or possibly lumber-shed, opposite our house no longer existed; a shell had wiped it off the earth. The house itself was standing drunkenly on three walls; the fourth had been shot away. About a hundred yards beyond, houses and trees were burning close to the church.

A few paces from the house a British artilleryman was lying dead. Death had overtaken him just as he was taking shelter from it. His back was ploughed with shrapnel, and he still had his mess-tin in his right hand. One of his comrades collected his pay-book and documents from his pockets. Among the papers were several photographs, some letters, but little else. Those who returned would hand these things in to the adjutant. Someone somewhere in Britain would receive a long yellow envelope with the words "On His Majesty's service," and in it would be these letters, photographs, papers … .

But we had no time for meditation, or for funeral solemnities. Close by the crimson patch of a parachute was lying; it had been used to drop supplies yesterday. We shifted the dead man a little off the path, that he might be no hindrance to the living, and covered him with the parachute.

One of our wireless operators was seriously wounded in the lungs, the left shoulder and thigh. He was diving under a jeep when he was hit. He smiled wanly and asked to be pardoned for not saving the apparatus. It was lying beside him in fragments.

We went back to the accompaniment of German artillery. Here and there roofs crumbled down on the village houses, here and there trees crashed down in the forest. The road was crowded with civilians, who were running helplessly in both directions: east and west. To Arnhem and away from Arnhem. Weeping women were desperately wringing their hands and asking us by signs where they were to go. As if we knew. Surely better to go eastward, to get away from Arnhem; but could one be sure of anything now?

We made our way a second time through the forest from Oosterbeek to Hartenstein. We again passed a group of houses on the edge of the forest; one of them was gone now. A form lay motionless by the wicket-gate. By the clothing I recognised the stout Dutch woman who had only that morning asked me: "Is anything serious going to happen here?" My thoughtless optimism had proved to be a criminal mistake.

After going on for some time we realised that we could go no further. It would be madness to try. Everything around us was quivering and every tree was rocking as though it would fall at any moment. We saw a few lonely trenches among the bushes to one side of the road. We crawled through the bushes and heard the invitation:

"Come in with us. You're safer in than on the earth."

They were holding part of the glider-pilots' positions. We gladly accepted their invitation. The fire was growing heavier with every minute.

"How far is the Second Army? Have the Poles arrived?" our hosts asked us.

That was the first time I heard a question about the Second Army. I didn't know that from now onward the question would be repeated again and again, because the Second Army was now the basis of all hope, and that the words "The Second Army is coming" would even at the worst moment justify faith in their being rescued and their hope of aid.

We squatted down on the floor of the trenches, from time to time scraping off the earth which sprinkled over our tin hats and overalls. The trees bowed towards the ground as though before a storm, and the air was rent incessantly with the whistle and groan of shells.

I saw two worms crawling under the root of a tree in front of me. They reached the smooth surface of the yellow earth and slipped into it with slow, but decided movements. "They're not troubled by bomb problems", the idiotic thought entered my head. But as for us, we could not get away from the crash of explosions in the forest. Every tree multiplied the tumult. The echoes flew from bush to bush. And even when we were sure the shells were not falling in our neighbourhood the sound of their explosion was so terrific that it stunned one's mind and prevented all logical thought.

But now a rending cry arose above even the roar of the artillery. We started up in our trenches.

A large group of children came running through the trees, stumbling against the bushes, tripping over the hummocks and ditches. There were at least ten of them, and possibly more. A girl in her teens, a typical flapper, was in charge of the band. A group of little Dutch children, the oldest probably not more than ten, ran behind her. How had they got into the forest? Whom were they running away from, or whom had they been separated from? Why were they alone?

We had no idea. We couldn't help them. We were quite helpless. For a moment we wondered whether to take them into our trenches, but we rejected the suggestion. The military principle, 'no one must be held', determined our decision, for who knew whether the shells might come crashing into our trenches at any moment? So we only shouted to them and pointed the way they should go. Let them get on to the main road. There they would find grown-ups, and houses; they could take shelter in the cellars. And here there was only the forest. No, not only the forest, but also a presence moving towards us slowly but inexorably, a presence who would ere long become the sole and exclusive master of this forest.

Even the children's shouts heralded the coming of that presence, the coming of death.

The Bet

In the afternoon we went out to meet the Polish Brigade. "We must take a jeep for the general to travel back to the Divisional Command in," said one of our officers.

"It seems to me," I ventured to remark," that at least as important as a jeep would be a duck, or a raft at any rate.The general can't cross the Lek in a jeep."

"I don't regard that as a problem. There's a ferry where we're going, and we must take it for granted that our lads have managed to capture 'it'. Of course, the ferry may not wait for our arrival, but we'll take the optimistic view," someone explained.

We drove in a jeep through the forest, and the driver dodged trees and bushes like a truck driver. The lighter line of the Bren gun in front striped the car's greyish-brown paint. The barrels of Sten guns gleamed dully from the sides. We were a little mobile fortress and we would give a good account of ourselves if need be.

At the command of the Airlanding Brigade we were given a guide and lots of apples. The staff, sitting in trenches under trees, encouraged us to proceed.

"Your men will be of great assistance to us. It's getting more and more difficult to make a counter-attack, and we're beginning to get rather short of men even for defence," one of the officers said.

About a mile and half from Oosterbeek there is a tram terminus on the main road; there a tram No. 12 was standing with windows smashed and, of course, with no passengers. I wondered whether they had managed to get back to Arnhem. Close to the terminus we turned off to the left to the headquarters of a British battalion.

At that moment two men in civilian dress ran out of the forest and halted our car just as we were turning off the road. One of them tried to explain something to us in a guttural voice, speaking a language which he evidently thought was English. We did not understand what he was saying, and we hadn't time to find out. The driver started up the car, but the other civilian seized the steering wheel. The situation looked awkward. It looked as if the two civilians intended to attack us, but surely they wouldn't dare to attack a jeep full of men and guns?

Slowly, with the aid of gestures, we discovered what the matter was. They were Dutch, and had come across two British soldiers who had escaped after being captured by the Germans. They were close by. Of course, the best plan would be for them to go with us, for our posts were not far away.

Now more machines were flying over, dropping supplies, and once more the German artillery burst into fury. The noise was even greater, if possible, than it had been in the morning.

"If your lads are given such a welcome … ", the battalion commander did not finish his sentence.

He was right. It was inconceivable that the Brigade could land safely in such conditions.

We doubled along the sides of a ravine, clinging to the undergrowth and bushes, sheltering from the enemy observation posts. Here the British positions were held fairly strongly. From the top of a steep rise, down to the bank of the river. But the enemy held positions somewhere right behind them. He could observe all the roads and crossings. He could fire as he wished and, I must admit, made plentiful use of his possibilities. We were in one of the most amazing sectors held by the Airborne Division, no one knew who was surrounded or by whom, and it was difficult to say who had the upper hand.

On the long steps with innumerable stairs which led from the foot to the top of the rise, we came across a group of British officers. Among them were two or three Scots, who were delighted to see "kinsmen" visiting their positions. For Poles also "come" from Scotland.

"Glasgow's my native town, and I had the pleasure of meeting Poles there in 1940," said a tall captain.

"I don't regard Glasgow as the most beautiful city in the world," I answered; "but I'd be glad to be there at this moment."

They agreed with faint smiles. We lit cigarettes, and unanimously came to the conclusion that one can get used to anything. The German artillery fire had not diminished at all, but somehow our nerves had "settled down."

I crawled a little farther down, made myself comfortable under a bush and enjoyed the hospitality of the soldiers in the trenches. I was given biscuits and chewing gum. Someone even gave me a mess tin of water, which was growing very scarce in Hartenstein.

Before us stretched the green of the riverside meadow and the blue of the Lek. A large embankment led to the spot where the ferry had been only recently. Now it was gone. We could clearly see that the jetty had been blown up, and saw the tops of the wooden piles sticking out of the water.[1]

"Well, in that case even a dog couldn't get across," the British officers declared. "Our men are in those bushes leading down to the river. They're holding the bank and the immediate area. On the other hand the river and especially the approach to the ferry are under enemy fire."

That moment something happened which provided ocular confirmation of this estimate of the position. In a trench at the roadside two soldiers made a bet of a very unusual and even original kind. I could hear their raised voices.

"You see, I'll bring in that box of supplies which fell in the meadow," said one of them …

The box with its parachute lay on an open stretch of meadow some fifteen yards from the embankment and the bushes which masked our positions.

"It can't be done," the other answered. "A fly couldn't settle there."

"Bet me a packet of Players?"

"Okay, but I'll be sorry for you."

"Don't you worry about me!"

The stake was high: a packet of Players was a small fortune to us now.

An agile, athletic figure ran quickly across the road and dashed into the bushes, coming out again suddenly on the embankment some dozens of yards farther on. There was a crash, and the clatter of automatic pistols. Spandaus chattered ominously. The Germans certainly controlled the bank. Bullets sped after the Britisher, tried to overtake him in the meadow, fell all around him. But he was determined to win his bet. He made two great bounds and dropped

---

1 Before leaving England General Sosabowski had been told of his Brigade's new DZ and that it should use the Heveadorp ferry to cross the river and reinforce those troops fighting north of the Rhine. This ferry was not mentioned in the plans for Market Garden as it was assumed the bridges would be captured intact, and this somewhat insignificant and small ferry was brushed aside. When the Oosterbeek perimeter started forming on the Tuesday and Wednesday it was based on the positions units were in at that time. Regretfully little thought was given as to where it could be best located for the future benefit of the operation. After the Arnhem road bridge had been lost, possibly the most important feature was this ferry, which was under the Westerbouwing heights, at the extreme western end of the perimeter. The ferry had been operating normally until this Wednesday; indeed it had taken men and equipment from several gliders who had landed south of the Rhine across to join up with their comrades. However, on this day the ferryman Pieter Hensen decided to cut the cable on the south bank to deny the use of the ferry to the Germans and later sank the ferry near the north bank. The most important point to remember about this area was that it was one of the few places, if not *the* only place, where roads came right up to the river bank on both sides. If 2nd Army had reached this area it is possible men could have been put across. If the area had been more securely held, perhaps with the Westerbouwing as the kingpin of the defence, a Bailey bridge may have been able to be built under the protection of men on the northern bank and the momentum of Market Garden maintained. As it was the strategic importance of the Westerbouwing heights and the ferry were ignored until it was too late.

beside the box. With a large knife he cut the ropes of the parachute and crawled back on his return journey. He crawled because the box was heavy, and there could be no thought of running. In addition he had to crawl in zigzags, to make it as difficult as possible for the enemy.

The sight was unnerving. I lit a cigarette, and was filled with anger. I could have used my fists on those two men.

"These sportsmen, damn them!" I cursed louder and louder. "Must have something to bet about!"

The man who looked like losing the bet turned his head towards me and laughed at my state of nerves.

"Don't you worry!" he said, "it looks as if I've lost."

The other man was now crawling along the embankment. It was not very wide, and an easy mark to aim at. So he made one great effort, flung the box on to his shoulders and ran the last few yards like a streak of light. In a couple of seconds or so he had vanished into the bushes.

The machine-guns died away. No point in wasting ammunition. This British-German match was finished. A score of one-nil to the British.

Someone ran behind us swiftly downhill, repeating the news we had already heard once that day: "Your Brigade won't be coming today. Weather conditions won't allow of their starting from England."

"Well, it can't be helped, we'll have to go back," we said.

"But they may come tomorrow. I'm quite sure we'll be coming out here again tomorrow to meet them," I remarked.

Of course, this time too I'd be wrong in my expectations. I did not really expect that it would be possible for them to arrive here tomorrow, for tomorrow the Germans would be here.

The Artillery Takes a Hand

I spent Wednesday night in a very nomadic manner. I am not fond of trenches, and I can't stand the cold. I was not attached to any force and I had no obligations. I took advantage of the favourable position of a war correspondent, a man who is of no necessity to anybody, and so can wander where he pleases. Yet I felt ashamed to go down into the cellar. Despite my colleagues' advice, I decided to go on sleeping in one of the rooms. On the first floor, of course. The ground floor was occupied by the Divisional Command; and the second floor was decidedly unencouraging. I groped my way from room to room, trying to decide which was the safest. The rooms were empty and dark. Outside from time to time the red gleam of flying shrapnel streaked the sky. The beds were without mattresses or blankets, for everything had been taken down into the cellar for the wounded.

Finally I chose a room looking on to the forest. I had my army blanket with me; I lay down on the slats of one of the beds and fell asleep almost at once. But I was very soon awakened by the sound of trees crashing and an explosion. Then a second and a third. The window-glass rattled suspiciously, so I shifted to another room on the other side of the house. But I had hardly stretched myself out on the bed when pieces of glass flew on to my blanket.

I gave up the idea of a bed and sheltered on the floor in one corner. But there it was very cold and very uncomfortable. So I went out into the corridor, where there was a huge bookcase half let into the wall. I behaved like a barbarian, for I shifted a whole pile of stoutly bound volumes from the lowest shelf and crawled into the space I had cleared.

"A real man in his rightful place," I whispered proudly, and this time fell sound asleep.

On Thursday morning the Divisional Command shifted to the cellars. The ground floor now had no windows and the chandeliers were hanging very precariously from the ceilings. The walls were cracked and crumbling, and the general effect was far from reassuring.

In the hotel's former reception hall, now empty and inhospitable, a small table with a map spread over it was being set up. The Divisional Commander, General Urquhart, was about to talk to the war correspondents.

German prisoners taken by Poles.

German Prisoners taken by the Poles. It is believed the two 'Germans' on the left were Poles in Wehrmacht service. On the right is Lieutenant J. Dyrda, Sosabowski's Adjutant and Interpreter.

A German prisoner at work.

This photograph is believed to have been taken in the Driel area.

German prisoners rounded up by British paratroopers.
A picture taken by Sergeant M. Lewis on 18th September in the garden of a house on the corner of Hogenkampseweg and Bennekomseweg near Heelsum. The men are most likely from D Company of the 1st Borders. This house was pulled down in the 1980s.

Several of us sat around the table. The General began his explanation of the situation. He discussed the position, as it had existed on the first day, apparently favourable, yet containing the germs of serious complications in the future. The Division was quite alone on the northern bank of the Lek—the lower Rhine. From the beginning it was difficult for us to capture Arnhem, and now it was out of the question. The Germans were in a position to bring up continual reinforcements; we had got to wait till the Second Army, which was fighting its way through to Nijmegen, had reached us.

"At this moment," the General pointed to the map, "practically speaking we're surrounded. But things aren't so very bad, for only comparatively small enemy forces are opposing us. But they deprive us of our power of manoeuvre, and are forcing us to stay put. But considerable German forces are approaching us from here," he ran his hand over the map and pointed to two large blue rings to the west of us but to the north of Arnhem." They're some miles away yet; they're marching through areas held by their own men. They may be in our

The Germans who tried to infiltrate through the Airborne forces lines, but were killed by Sten Gun fire.

The photo shows two dead Germans who were killed on the night of 20th/21st September by C Company of the Border Regiment, trying to infiltrate Airborne forces lines in the Van Lennepweg area in Oosterbeek. This shot was taken by Sergeant D. Smith of the A.F.P.U.

area today, certainly tomorrow. Then our situation will be difficult. The more so as the position in regard to supplies doesn't seem to be too good, though the air force can't do any more than it is doing. In any case, so far as the future's concerned either everything will clear up in our favour by Sunday, or. . . . At the moment I have quite a handful of men in immediate reserve for our defence, and of course, a few war correspondents," the general laughed.

Shrapnel was whistling outside the hotel. Today we could hear the fire of machine-guns, too. The Germans were quite close. A machine-gun bullet ricocheted off the window-frame, filling the room with its whistle. Another burst struck the corner of the house. We sat right opposite the large doors, which were wide open to the terrace. The General was completely unconcerned. With an easy smile on his face, he dispassionately explained and dealt with the situation as though he were in a lecture hall.

Supplies being dropped by parachute to the Airborne forces.

"It's a fine picture, and very instructive from the military aspect," he said, pointing again to the map.

"But when will the Polish Brigade arrive, sir?" I asked.

"The Poles were to have arrived on Tuesday. Then we expected them on Wednesday. Now we expect them today. We've been informed that bad weather is making it impossible for them to leave England. I'd be very glad to see them," General Urquhart answered.[1]

We got up and thanked him for his explanations. He said goodbye, and wished us success in our work.

I found Johnny Cotterill in a trench among the trees. I needed him badly at that moment as a kind of "private translator."

"Look, Johnny," I said, "my English isn't of the best, and I ought to send off a long dispatch. So ... "

1 This was now Thursday 21st September and the P.P.B. was two days late. Back in England the men left early for the airfields, and in spite of mist visibility seemed better, there was an encouraging forecast from the weather men and take-off was scheduled for 1200. Major-General Sosabowski received a message via the senior British liaison officer, Lieutenant Colonel Stevens, from Major-General Urquhart. This stated that his drop zone remained near Driel and the ferry was still in British hands.

Ammunition and supplies dropped by parachute are picked up.

Removing the straps from a recovered pannier after a successful resupply mission. This picture was taken by Sergeant D. Smith on 18th September in the Wolfheze area. The pannier contained 6-pounder ammunition and the man without the helmet undoing the straps is S/Sergeant McGeough of C Squadron G.P.R., the helmeted man to his right is C.Q.M.S. Holderness of 250 Company R.A.S.C.

"All right, Marek," he interrupted me. "But where shall we write it?"

We had to change our room time after time, interrupting our labours after almost every sentence. Mortar shells were dropping anywhere and everywhere. They broke into our conversation, spoilt our most effective sentences, and obscured the situation which, though far from justifying optimism, was at least clear before. Finally, we decided to take no notice of them. Let them do as they like, my despatch must go off to London. Our agreement muffled the explosions and we began to feel almost perfectly at ease . . . when the Germans began to range their artillery. The shell which had burst not far from the hotel terrace a minute ago was an artillery shell. Not mortar fire!

"If they go on like that they may bring the roof down on our heads," I said.

"But we must finish the dispatch," Johnny muttered, pre-occupied with his job as a translator.

A second shell fell almost as close as the first.

"It's a fine and instructive picture, General Urquhart declared today at a conference with war correspondents," my dispatch ended.

Now I had got to find Major Oliver.

When Modern Technique Fails

"I hope this will be our last attempt," we reassured one another that Thursday afternoon, when fate and duty commanded us to set out once more from Hartenstein to see the Polish parachutists arrive.

This one-sided, triple attempt to make a rendezvous with the Polish Brigade was beginning to be tiresome. The most capricious of girls had never kept us waiting so long for her arrival as had our own native unit. We knew that it was not their fault, our men would be only too glad to get here as quickly as possible. We realised how long the hours and days of waiting must seem to them, how unnerving it was to be in a state of continual readiness. But war is not governed by good wishes or by soldiers' desires. Somewhere among the higher-ups of the army, or possibly higher still, all the possibilities and conditions were being coldly and objectively considered. If the weather was bad and complicated the operation, obviously the flight must be called off.

"Your brigade will arrive today for certain. We know it's started from England," Colonel Preston assured us.[1]

Fine! We'd had enough of this hanging and dragging about.

"Keep a good lookout for snipers!" we were warned by men who had just returned from reconnoitring the terrain.

Good advice! The German approach to our positions was adding further complications. Snipers seemed to be everywhere. They testified to their presence even in the immediate neighbourhood of the Divisional Command, with single shots which went continually echoing through the forest. Where the snipers' positions were exactly, that, unfortunately, no one knew. The bullets which sped past our ears might be intended for us. We ran to the edge of the road. We stole along beside the bushes, only to realise after some time that the shots were not intended for us after all, that they were aimed somewhere near at hand. The hundred-mouthed echo of the forest had led us into error, as usual.

A British patrol came out of the trees on to the road. They halted, adjusted their equipment, looked about them and swore very loud.

---

1 Lieutenant Colonel P. Preston was Assistant Adjutant and Quartermaster General HQ 1st Airborne Division.

"There's a sniper at work on the edge of the forest a couple of hundred yards from here," the commander informed us.

"Probably in the last house on the left," another of the patrol added.

"I don't think so," the commander contradicted him "I think he's in a tree on the right."

A stupid business! Even within the small oval of our defence perimeter we did not have freedom of movement. The snipers had taken up positions on all the most important of our lines of communication: the Divisional Command to the Airlanding Brigade's positions, the artillery positions to the river. Their selection of spots was itself a proof that they had a good idea of our positions, that they had exact information about us.

We slowly drew near the dangerous spot. The trees of the forest ended and we saw the grey line of the high road. As though of malice, at this very moment the artillery and mortars took a rest. The sudden silence rendered the snipers' task easier. Our every step clattered on the asphalt of the forest road. But if we turned off it innumerable branches half severed by shells went cracking down, and the leaves rustled.

At the edge of the forest we drew up a plan to dart across the road. One by one, of course. Captain Zwolanski was the first to cross. A short burst from an automatic pistol snapped after him. Then ran Lieutenant Pronobis, then I, then the liaison men.[2] We chose the straightest road possible, counting, as we said, on the sniper's "regulation " psychology. He would certainly expect our plan to be cunning and complicated. That we would take a roundabout route, that we would try running in two's, or three's, that we would scatter all over the road like a flock of bewildered sheep. And so he would surely cover quite a long strip of road with shots. He would put down almost a barrage and, trying to achieve too much, would achieve nothing ... All six of us successfully vanished over a rise into the bushes, and now we felt quite safe.

Too soon! As we approached the first houses of Oosterbeek the Germans spotted us again and reminded us of their existence. This time shots from an automatic pistol sprinkled over the three or four small trenches into which we tumbled with our equipment. While we were in this shelter Captain M. looked over a hedge and called to us. He had come from the artillery positions, where he was spending all his days.

"I'm going to liquidate that swine! I've just about had enough of all this," he

2 Lieutenant A. Pronobis was one of several liaison officers at the HQ P.P.B.

Captain Ludwik Zwolanski, who swam across the river with the message from General Urquhart to General Sosabowski.

said in an irritated tone.

"Can anyone go with you?" we asked.

"No, I don't want any help," he answered categorically. "The sniper's alone and he must be dealt with by a man acting singly. One makes less noise, and I've got an equal chance: one against one."

He jumped through the hedge. All we could see of him was the bushes swaying at times along his route.

"The joker was in the corner house," he told us when he returned an hour later. "He defended himself a bit, but not much. We can take this road in safety now."

We made our way along the slope of a long and high embankment above the river, right past the artillery positions. Two soldiers were playing poker in a circular trench beside a gun. Several others had gone off to a narrow ditch and were washing the soot and mud off their faces in the dirty water. We were used to the trick, long since established among the British troops, of blacking and greasing their faces so that they shouldn't show up and should have a better effect on the enemy when they met him. But it gave a lot of trouble when it had to be washed off.

The roar of aeroplanes approached from the south. It grew louder and louder, until it rose into the regular throb of squadrons of Spitfires which appeared out of the clouds. They circled the opposite bank once, twice, then swooped down and swept the German positions with fire. So they were softening up the German defence! They were pinning the enemy to the ground in order to make the Brigade's landing possible.

The German artillery was mostly on our northern side of the River Lek. The bulk of their forces on the southern side consisted of infantry. On the ground machine-guns stuttered with considerable spite but with little effect. The artillery tried to shift its fire to cover the southern bank. But that required time. At the moment the Spitfires had un-challengeable supremacy.

Into this fiery discussion between heaven and earth entered a new, very tumultuous, roar of engines, stronger than before. Dakotas now came up behind the Spitfires. From where we were standing we could see only part of the force, and that a small part. They circled above the meadow and reduced speed. They were low above the ground. Below the first Dakota one parachute, then another, a third, opened up. The Polish parachutists were jumping.[3]

3 In England as 1200 approached there seemed to be no improvement in the weather and the take-off time was again postponed. Then after another bout of 'dislocation of expectation' word came thorough that they were going. So at around 1400 at Saltby and Spanhoe the engines of 114 Dakotas burst into life – off at last! These aircraft from the 314th and 315th Troop Carrier Groups carried 1,568 paratroopers. The American pilots encountered much difficulty climbing through the cloud and then attempting to join up into their formations. It is recorded that one man jumped over Cambridgeshire but he went on a later lift. Then Murphy's Airborne Law came into play again – to those on the ground it seemed the weather was getting worse and it was decided to recall the aircraft before landing conditions became too dangerous. The radio operators in the aircraft had been given a different set of code words than those used by the ground stations. Four times the recall code was sent and it was almost a decision by individual pilots as to what the code meant. 41 of the Dakotas turned back and most landed at the first airfield they found as they descended through the cloud. It also appears one aircraft landed in Ireland. Of these 41 aircraft, 25 carried men of the 1st Battalion, 2 had 2nd Battalion passengers, and 11 carried men of the 3rd Battalion and 3 with Brigade H.Q. men.

The remaining 73 aircraft carried on using a route flying over Belgium. One Dakota carrying Brigade HQ personnel was damaged by flak when it strayed over German lines and it turned back into Belgium, dropping its troops there before returning to England. The drop started on DZ K about 1700, and was a messy affair. There were Germans around the DZ and the men came under fire. The American aircrews complained that the Poles were too slow in jumping; the Poles complained that they had been thrown about too much by evasive action. 5 aircraft from the 315th Troop Carrier Group were shot down but all the paratroopers jumped safely before the aircraft crashed. 10 American aircrew were killed, with more wounded and taken prisoner. It is thought that 1,003 men landed on and around DZ K with 5 men killed and 25 wounded, either during the drop

A PIAT gun in position behind a tree covering a road.

One of the more famous Arnhem photographs, taken by Sergeant D. Smith on the morning of 18th September 1944 in Wolfheze. It shows three men from the 1st Airborne Reconnaissance Squadron on the Duitsekampweg. Manning the PIAT in the middle is Trooper Jimmy Cooke and kneeling next to him is Trooper Ray Evans, both from H.Q. Troop. Further up the road by the level crossing sign is Trooper Fred Brawn of C Troop. The light railway line here was built by the Germans in 1941 to connect Wolfheze station to the airfield at Deelen some miles to the north. The track (no rail etc.) is partly visible as well as the small but high tunnel under the A12 motorway.

I felt hot all over. If the Germans were to break out and attack now, our parachutists would share the fate of the gliders. The high opposite bank of the Rhine, and especially the high embankment, which stretched parallel with the river line, prevented our seeing anything. We heard only a heavy and varied firing, but we could not decide who was firing at whom. Whether the Spitfires

or later that day. Not a good start.

As he had been told in England, Sosabowski rallied his men and sent the 2nd Battalion to secure the ferry area and the 3rd to a point opposite the Old Church in Oosterbeek. In the village of Driel Sosabowski met with some locals who informed him that the ferry was out of action. He is said to have commented, "How can it have gone in just a few hours?" It should also be added that the lone platoon from C Company of the 1st Borders which had been sent to hold the Westerbouwing heights had been attacked and overrun, leaving the ferry site completely unprotected.

Wounded British paratroop is carried away to the Hartenstein Hotel.

The man on the stretcher is Captain G. Hemelryk of the Divisional Signals Company; his role was nominally Cypher Officer, but on the day this picture was taken (Sunday 24th September) he had been on a supply recovery mission when he was wounded. Partly obscured at the front of the stretcher are L/Sergeant J. Rate and L/Corporal R. McFarlane, whilst at the back wearing a beret is Signaller F. Young and Signaller R. Gordon-Macintosh. The picture was taken close to the Hartenstein, and Hemelryk is being taken to the basement R.A.P.

at the Germans, or the parachutists at the Germans, or the Germans at the Spitfires and parachutists.

The main thing was that the Brigade was landing. We carried our wireless apparatus closer to the river and set it up.

"Hallo, Cuba, hallo, Cuba, this is Roman speaking. Can you hear me? Hallo, Cuba … " Ensign Pajak monotonously repeated.

But "Cuba " gave no sign of life. There was no answer. The time passed, dusk fell, and our agitation grew and grew. The orders from the Divisional Command were simple make contact as quickly as possible with the Polish Brigade. Besides, we knew that the Brigade's situation was not one to be envious of. They had landed in the midst of the German positions. They were far from the Second Army, at least ten miles, and they were separated from us by the river. What was their task? Obviously, to help us, and that as quickly as possible. But how? And in which direction?

The time passed inexorably and, as always in such situations, very quickly. We all sat around the wireless apparatus and waited another half hour, another hour. At last we could wait no longer. The Brigade's liaison officer attached to the Airborne Division Command, Captain Zwolanski, said:

"I'll get across the river. Only find me a boat of some sort."

That was the point: there wasn't a boat anywhere.

Neither on the bank, nor in the village, nor among the artillery. The sappers might have something that would do, but it was too late to look for them. And it was too late to knock anything together on which to cross. Time, time … time was the all-important factor. Minutes were very dear, hours were, priceless.

Captain Zwolanski decided:

"I'll swim across the river."

He went off to the battery command, removed his uniform, put on some camouflage netting to make it as easy, and, despite everything, as dry a crossing as possible. He decided to swim across at the spot where the ferry started. The Brigade would certainly make its way in that direction to look for possibilities of crossing to our bank. That was a very difficult operation, for all the crossings were in German hands.

Now began hours of long waiting. Would he find the Brigade or not? was the question which filled all our minds.

The German artillery shifted its fire to the other bank. Shells flew over us, causing fire after fire on the opposite side. Houses went up in flames, and it grew lighter and lighter. On our side, only mortars were firing against us now. The trajectory of their shells was always the same … Hartenstein, the road to Oosterbeek, and our artillery positions on the riverside meadow.

We packed ourselves into the cellar of one of the houses. The artillerymen were asleep, one beside another, in an incredibly cramped and stifling atmosphere, in the two damp rooms. We set up several boxes, to avoid sitting on the earth with its mud and water. The shells of mortars whistled and groaned over the house and all the village. They were falling very close, and the house shook and swayed like a cradle every moment. It was of such poor construction that it would present no problem even to mortar shells. They only had to hit it . . . .

So we waited in this cellar, in perfect darkness, and thought only: Did he get across, or not? Has he found General Sosabowski? For so much depended on the answers to these questions. Possibly everything. If the Brigade got across to us it would enable us to continue our resistance for a longer time. It would help us to hold out, and now it was all-important to hold out. It was all a matter of hours, or of a day at the most. It was a race with time, a race for time.

"General Urquhart said that if the situation isn't cleared by Sunday . . . ." I broke the general silence.

"Why shouldn't it be cleared by Sunday?" someone else interrupted. "The Second Army may arrive before then. In fact it ought to. Today's only Thursday."

"Let's say the night from Thursday to Friday," I corrected him, "and that leaves us . . . ."

The door creaked loudly and piercingly on its rusty hinges. Ensign Pajak entered, to tell us that...there was still no radio contact with the Brigade.

"He must have got across, for they didn't fire at him," Lieutenant Pronobis returned to the question which we were all pondering.

"He may have run into the Boches," Captain M. said soberly.

The box on which I was sitting was made of thin boards and was not used to being utilised as a chair. It suddenly broke down, and I fell inside it. There was the sound of breaking glass, and something thick and sticky began to soak through my uniform.

"Damn, it's jam!" I ascertained by the light of a lantern "And I'm sitting on cucumbers," Pronobis rejoiced.

We took out our knives and ate jam with cucumbers. Not a particularly appetising mixture, but we hadn't had any supper. Or dinner. Or breakfast.

Something more powerful than mortars began to drop things in our area. We shifted away from the "captured" jam, and listened closely. Yes, it was definitely artillery. Had they transferred their fire from Hartenstein to Oosterbeek?

"Good God!" Captain M. suddenly groaned: "That's our artillery giving us a dose."

And he ran to the battery command, to wireless for our over-enthusiastic neighbours to stop their fire. A few minutes later only the mortars were plaguing Oosterbeek.

"It would be amusing to get a British shell right on top of us," we said, rejoicing for quite inexplicable reasons.

The night was passing into a pale and anaemic morning when Captain Zwolanski turned up. He was tired, but in very good humour. He looked rather strange, for he was dressed in Dutch civilian attire. He had re-crossed the river by boat, and was happy, as his journey had been successful. He had found the Brigade not far from the ferry. He had seen the General and reported to him. Now at least things should go better. But …

"But what?" we asked.[4]

"The Brigade has got only two battalions," he said. "Nothing is known of the rest.[5] And besides, our men are hotly engaged. The Germans are pressing on them, our Brigade is counter-attacking, and we're all waiting to see what happens. Today they'll look for means of crossing, and tonight they'll come across to our side."

"What was the swim in the river like?" I passed to personal matters.

"Not very pleasant. The water was so devilishly cold that at first I groaned, and I all but choked. And the Germans fired at me a bit."

4 On 23rd September the remnants of the P.P.B. took off from Spanhoe heading for Holland. In all 41 Dakotas from the 315th T.C.G. carrying 560 troops, mostly from the 1st Battalion, headed for Holland. Their DZ was not around Driel but south of the Waal at Overasselt, in the 82nd U.S. Airborne Division's sector. Airborne Corps H.Q. had decided that they would go the rest of the way by road. It is believed every single aircraft made it to the DZ (which had been previously used as LZ O for U.S. gliders) and it was virtually an 'exercise jump'. From Overasselt the Poles moved to the Groesbeek area spent the night here and arrived in the Driel area the following day. It would seem Marek got his dates mixed up slightly as the first lift of the P.P.B. landed on the 21st and the second group on the 23rd.

5 Author: We learned later that part of the Brigade landed elsewhere, and linked up with the main force only on the following day.

From the South to the North Bank

The hotel was gone. The comfortable roofs, the soft mattresses, the windows with fine views on to the forest, the flowerbeds and the road, were gone. There was rubble in the rooms, window-frames with no glass in them hung uselessly, pieces of broken furniture were scattered over the floors. Snipers were firing into the doorless hotel vestibule. Under cover of night they had made their way through our outposts, under dozens of fallen trees, and now were firing as they wished from the very heart of the Airborne Division's positions.

It was difficult to be sure where the snipers were, just as it was difficult to distinguish one shot from another, ours from theirs, or the shrapnel of mortars from the explosions of artillery. The only distinctive sound was made by what seemed to be a new weapon being used by the Germans. Its explosions were deceptively like the clapping of hands. That clapping was inhuman: it came after a hit, after some cry, after someone's death. It sounded as if someone above were watching the forest of Hartenstein in delight at the masterly game being played.

And the German game was certainly being played well more and more men lay forever in the trenches where they had sheltered. One couldn't bury them, for there was no time or possibility. To bury one's colleagues one would have to get out of the trench and expose oneself to shells, to fragments, to shrapnel. At the most, if all the men in a trench ceased to live, their neighbours mercifully jumped out and with a few hurried movements shovelled the earth down … and that was all. So trenches with living, fighting men were in close proximity to the improvised collective graves.

The casualty figures were rising alarmingly. The narrow and confined cellars of the hotel contained fresh groups of wounded after each burst of bombardment and shells. The staff worked on amid the wounded. And, strange to say, though the wounded were suffering, and the staff was faced with a task surpassing human possibility, the atmosphere in the cellar was calm, steady, and inexorable. Yes, inexorable.

"What do you think of me, sir? Shall I get well?" a sergeant-major just brought in from the trenches asked. Spandau bullets had ripped open his belly just as he was rising and about to leap out of the trench. Now he was slowly dying from loss of blood.

Along the narrow, crowded corridor men were passing continually, jostling the sergeant major's stretcher. The bandages, soaked with blood, had to be changed incessantly. Outside there was no break in the gunfire, and there was no possibility of transport for the wounded.

The doctor gave him a long look, and pondered even longer over his answer.[1]

"I'm afraid, sergeant-major," he said at last, slowly," that you're in a very bad way."

"But shall I live?"

"I'm very sorry, but I can hardly think so," the doctor said. The wounded man's situation was hopeless; the soldier was entitled to know all the truth.

The man looked into our faces, and was silent. A long silence. Long seconds, monstrously long seconds passed.

Someone fumbled in his pocket and pulled out a hopelessly crumpled cigarette, to lay it on the wounded man's blanket. The sergeant major did not light it, for he could not, but ... the cigarette was the only thing we could give him.

At last, with a great effort he raised his head from the stretcher and, gazing at us, whispered calmly

"All right sir, all right ... "

I did not note the sergeant major's name. It was one of those moments when it is difficult to remember one's professional duties. I know only that he did die. I am not sorry that I did not know his name. If I did know it, I would write something about a brave, fearless man named Smith, or Brown, or Ferguson. About one, individual man. But now that nameless sergeant has become for me an imperishable symbol of those many "Red Devils" who were truly not afraid of anything.

Not even death.

We had run out of cigarettes.

"There are only a few cigarettes and they're for the wounded," said the grey-

1 This doctor was Lieutenant D. Randall, who ran the R.A.P. in the basement of the Hartenstein Hotel. Officially his role was as Medical Officer to the H.Q. Royal Artillery but in reality he was R.M.O. to Divisional H.Q.

headed chaplain,[2] who was working as a volunteer in our hospital. He went out with the stretcher-bearers whenever it was quiet, to bring in the wounded from the trenches.

Nor had we anything to eat.

"This corned beef is only for the wounded," said the orderly in the kitchen as he opened tins of meat.

We had nothing to drink, and we were plagued with thirst.

"Water is only for the seriously wounded," the doctor said pleasantly enough, but decidedly.

Meanwhile the staff was faced with a very difficult problem, perhaps the most difficult of all in this campaign. How to bring the Polish Brigade over to our side? The assumptions and plans had been for them to land when the bridge over the Lek in the suburbs of Arnhem would be in our hands. That they would strike at the bridgehead on the southern bank, and then link up with the Airborne Division. And that, with the Airborne Division, they would go into a decisive attack.[3]

Now, of course, the whole situation had changed. Now the Brigade had only one task: to come to the aid of the Division. But how was it to get across to us?

An accident settled the question. It transpired that the sappers were in

---

2 This grey-haired chaplain was Padre A. Harlow, the senior chaplain for the 1st Airborne Division and his normal place of work was at H.Q. He is recorded as radiating calm and authority at the H.Q., while his white shock of hair was to be seen everywhere in and about the Hartenstein. His tranquillity and calmness had a positive effect on all present; his efforts did not go unnoticed as he was awarded a D.S.O. in 1945 for services at Arnhem. He often assisted Lieutenant Randall in the basement R.A.P. and on 24th September he visited the Tafelberg dressing station when it was occupied by a group of Waffen S.S. The Germans wanted to move around 150 walking wounded away under the leadership of a doctor or a chaplain. Major G. Rigby-Jones of 181 Airlanding Field Ambulance suggested that he might like to go. In spite of having previously been a POW in North Africa earlier in the war, he did not hesitate and accompanied them to the St. Elisabeth's Hospital in Arnhem.

3 Perhaps one of the greatest tragedies at Arnhem and indeed in Market Garden was the almost total lack of planning with regard to water crossings. Whilst it would be easy to blame the engineers at Arnhem for not taking boats, the amount of stores they could actually fit in their aircraft and gliders was limited. They had a difficult decision to make, as the medics had, when deciding which bits of kit they should leave behind. In the plan there were potentially three bridges at Arnhem that could have been taken to provide a crossing and I suppose the planners thought they would get at least one. However, the apparent lack of urgency in giving assault boats a priority in the XXX Corps snake is criminal. One would have thought that with six waterways at least to cross, boats and bridging equipment would need to be fairly near the front.

Perhaps the optimism of the plan can be summed up by the comment from a British liaison officer from 1st Airborne to Captain J. Lorys that the situation should be so well in hand by the time the P.P.B. arrived that they would be met 'in commandeered buses, bring us over the bridge into Arnhem and treat us to a cup of tea there.'

possession of two dinghies. They had come with gliders, which, instead of individual lifebelts, carried two-seat boats. Abandoned and left on one of the jeeps, the dinghies now became one of the bases for our optimism.[4]

In the evening Lieutenant Maclean came to me and asked whether we were really going by night across the river to bring the Polish soldiers over to our positions.

"Of course, we're going about ten o'clock," I answered.

"I want to go with you," said Maclean. "My colleagues, the glider-pilots also want to help. You won't mind, I suppose?"

Of course we didn't mind, on the contrary, we welcomed the unexpected help with enthusiasm. Captain Zwolanski at once set to work with Maclean to draw up a detailed plan – where posts would be established on the river bank, how to cross the meadow, and which way the force would march from Oosterbeek to their positions.

We all started out, for we had to pick up the glider pilots on the way. Maclean found one of his groups in the forest and disappeared into the darkness with them. We collected the further groups, sent them ahead to the river, and then went along ourselves.

During their flight the shells which began to speed over our heads gave off a roar and whistle which was the loudest we at Arnhem had heard. They burst a long way, perhaps a mile or even more, ahead of us, but the sound of their explosion was so great that involuntarily we stooped down every time one went over, and were unnerved by each explosion.

"That must be heavy artillery," I thought, and felt very, very uncomfortable. For, if the Germans already had heavy artillery, our fate was decided. We could endure, through not very happily, under mortar fire, we could in the last resort stand light artillery fire. But heavy artillery? One shell dropped on our positions would reduce the hotel at Hartenstein to dust, and the trenches to powder.

While I was thus meditating I fell with a crash over a fallen tree. In a moment the crack of an automatic pistol sounded somewhere above us. A sniper, damn him! He was firing blindly, guided only by ear. We had forgotten the snipers. We must move more quietly and cautiously.

For the first time in our wanderings we did not cut through Oosterbeek, but went down the road past the houses in the direction of the church, where

4 The story of the attempts to get the P.P.B. across the Rhine is a tragic one and I have included a small account of the efforts made on both sides as Appendix A.

we had arranged for the guides to assemble. It was almost as clear as daylight, for something was burning on the line of hills to the west of us. At that distance we could not be sure where the fire was, but it seemed to be in a suburb of Arnhem.

"A suburb of Arnhem?" I was inwardly surprised.

But the Germans are there. Our battalion is no longer holding the centre of the town. And besides, they wouldn't be able to start such a blaze."

The sounds of conversation reached us from under a wide-spreading tree. The tones sounded excited and rather jubilant. We went up, and found a group of our friends. Instead of greeting them I automatically ducked as a shell went whistling over at that very moment.

"What made you duck to the shells?" Captain M. said in surprise.[5] "That's the artillery of the Second Army's 30th Corps shelling the Germans from the other side of the river."[6]

So it was heavy artillery—but ours! Ours! And it was Arnhem they were firing at. That blaze was their work. For the first time the words "Second Army" began to take on material form, to have a vital content.

An hour later we went off to make the crossing. Rain was falling, the mud clung to our feet, I slipped about in the rich earth of vegetable plots, but all the same I tried to move as quietly as possible. In front of me Captain M. crept along like a cat, behind me and 2nd Lieutenant Majewski[7] was squelching along rather too noisily. We made our way into "No man's land," the riverside meadow. In the daytime it would be unwise to show oneself here, but the night concealed many follies with its darkness.

Darkness? But the night was by no means so dark as it ought to have been. The suburb of Arnhem was burning more and more brightly and clearly. And on the other side of the river a village was flaming. Judging by the map

5 These shells were fired from Nijmegen about 11 miles from Arnhem by guns of the 64th Medium Regiment Royal Artillery. Contact by radio was first established on 21st September around 0945 and the first fire support missions were passed across the link around 1030. The 64th had two batteries of 4.5 inch guns and one of 5.5. At this time the Regiment was located about 4 miles south of Nijmegen around 12½ miles from Oosterbeek. So great was the distance that the first two targets were beyond the range of the guns and so some of the guns were moved forward to a position close by the power station in Nijmegen, which meant the whole of the perimeter was in range. Once the advance group had settled in the others moved up. It is worth adding the weight of shell fired by the 75mm pack howitzers of the Divisional artillery weighed 15 pounds. Those arriving on the German positions fired from Nijmegen weighed 95 pounds. Many of the targets fired at over the coming days were within 150 yards of the perimeter positions and on two occasions fire was requested and arrived on areas inside the perimeter to try and break up parties of Germans who had infiltrated.

6 In fact it was firing not from across the Lek, but from beyond the River Waal.

7 2nd Lieutenant K. Majewski was commander of the 3rd Battalion's Anti-Tank Platoon.

it should be Driel, which was where the Polish Brigade was halted. The glare of these fires threw a broad reflection across the meadow, and, worst of all, across the river. In that monotonously red, rather dull light I could see large, awkward and extravagant outlines moving ahead of me. I heard groans, or sighs perhaps. Then something ran past to one side of us with a heavy stamp and a loud rustling noise.

Ah, now I had it. They were cows, the proverbial Dutch cows, turned out into the meadow by their owners, and lowing at almost every shell explosion. "In these conditions those cows are condemned to inevitable extermination," I told myself. (I could only talk to myself, for I had promised Captain M. that despite my garrulity I would not say a word to anyone during this journey.)

We passed a hedge, we were steadily descending a slope, the earth grew marshy, and then we were treading over ordinary riverside mud. We lay down behind one of the many stone embankments which keep the waters of the lower Rhine in their course, and took our bearings.

"There are some German machine-gun positions about three hundred yards to the left," Captain M. whispered, "and there are more Germans about half a mile to the right. You remain here". He turned to me, "and we'll take cover behind the next embankments, for we don't know exactly where the dinghies will cross. There'll be one of us behind each embankment: all we've got to do is to see that those who land make as little noise as possible and show themselves still less."

The two officers vanished into the red and blue twilight. I was alone. The artillery shells continued to whistle overhead, passing over at regular intervals, from the southern bank to the north and from the northern bank to the south. The artillerymen on both sides were putting up a good show, and evidently were giving the infantry a hot time.

I tried to memorise a picture of the meadow, its shape, peculiarities and characteristics, for I knew I would be writing of this crossing. I knew this was the first time I had set foot in the meadow, but I had no idea it would not be the last. Nor that I would be seeing it in a much more brilliant light and in incomparably worse conditions. Nor that along this same route I would be running amid a crowd of men whom the Germans thought they had condemned to death, during the night of our evacuation to the southern bank of the Lek.

Meanwhile, the glare of fires was laying a broad band of light over the river. With wedge after wedge, stripe after stripe of rosy colour across the dark blue waters. At a certain moment I saw a dark patch moving swiftly towards me along one of those stripes. I fixed my eyes on it. Yes, there was no doubt about it, it was a dinghy. It was not far off, some dozens of yards from our bank. I could see it perfectly, I could even see the oars dipping into the blue water, then glittering with a rosy reflection against the yellowish stripe of reflected light. But I could not hear any sound. I could not even hear the oars dipping into the water, or the ripple of water as the boat moved forward. It was very clear to see, almost spectral. Yet it was moving with the utmost caution.

From somewhere to my left a Spandau chattered in an unpleasant deep tone, firing a long burst of light shells. The night grew still lighter and I shivered unpleasantly, for an orange rocket went up after the shells.

Had they seen us?

No. Again all was quiet. They were bored, the devils, in their trenches, and were amusing themselves from time to time with fireworks. Letting us know they were still there. That they were on the watch.

And it seemed that the short bark of the Spandau on the left was not of any ominous importance to us, for a little later there was a similar performance to our right. A long barking burst and an orange rocket. And then silence. The Germans had not noticed anything suspicious.

The quiet, but audible splash of oars and the gurgling of water reported that they had arrived. They scrambled swiftly up the slippery stones of the embankment, their equipment clattering rather too noisily.

"Lie down!" I whispered. "We'll wait here for the next lot."

There were six of them. Quietly, one after another the first men from the other side lay down beside me. I quietly asked the nearest man about the Brigade.

"It's under fire," he answered briefly. "Rather heavy. They're all waiting to cross now."

"And how did the landing go?"

"More or less successfully. We were fired at from the ground, but apparently the Germans were taken by surprise. How are things here? "

"Not too bright. We've been waiting for you. But you'll soon see for yourselves."

The others leaned across their comrades, greedily listening to my words. They wanted to know everything, but this was not the moment for explanations. But I couldn't halt them in the telling of their own stories. In excited whispers they told how they had got thoroughly worked up because they hadn't been allowed to fly across, how they had begun to fear that they would be left out of the operation and how difficult were the days of waiting. How stupid it had been to have to climb out of the aeroplanes on to the same aerodrome from which they had started on Tuesday and Wednesday, instead of making the jump into Holland.

But now the next group was landing on the bank. We made our way along the embankment and went back to the meadow.

"Don't be alarmed at that snoring noise," I warned them. "It's only cows."

A machine-gun stuttered angrily behind us, and swiftly came to a stop. The fires in Arnhem were dying out, a rain was falling more and more heavily, it grew rather darker, and that encouraged us. The darkness concealed us from observation; the rain and the wet meadow would muffle our footsteps. We walked swiftly and confidently, and my optimism returned. There were more of us now, and tomorrow there would be still more. But how many would be able to get across during this one night? Two dinghies didn't provide much in the way of transport. If only the entire battalion managed to get across tonight!

A guard came out to us as we reached the artillery positions:

"All Poles are to go to the church and there wait to march off to positions."

The church porch was very dark, and as we made our way through it we stumbled and knocked against one another. But it was almost light in the nave. Although the distant fires were fading they threw a crimson glare through the windows, and by a strange chance the light fell on the high altar.

"It's all very queer," one of our men sitting beside me on the bench remarked. "All the time I'd been thinking we were going to fly to Warsaw. . . For you know . . .our standard. . . ."

"I know," I assented.

"Our standard's from Warsaw,"[8] he went on." Polish women made and

8 The P.P.B.'s standard was, as Marek said, made in Warsaw. Its origins came about when Colonel Sosabowski (as he was in 1941) asked some of the officers who had served in the Brigade but were returning to Poland as part of the Underground Army, that they ask people in Warsaw to 'present a proper Polish military standard to the Brigade.' It was Sosabowski's dream to return to the city with it. In late 1941 six men jumped into what they thought was Poland but landed in German annexed territory. Two of them were killed but the others escaped and their leader, Captain M. Kalenkiewicz, was wounded. They reached Warsaw and whilst he was recovering from his wounds he met with some women and told them of the desire for a standard. This idea was acted upon and a standard manufactured. It had added significance as it used the ruby-red silk robe of Cardinal Dunajewski, a 19th century Polish patriot, which was donated to the cause. After nearly a year it was finished. It was designed in the traditional pattern for Polish military standards; a red Maltese cross on a white field. One side bore the Polish eagle and the arms of Warsaw. The other had St Michael the Archangel (the patron saint of paratroopers) embroidered in the centre. Above this image were the words 'Warszawa 1942' and below this 'Surge, Polonia' ('Arise, Poland'). On both sides in each

embroidered it. It was carried to Scotland across frontier after frontier. And they remembered the standard, for when the rising broke out in Warsaw in August they said in the despatches that they were waiting for us. That their standard would bring our Brigade to their help. I thought I'd be seeing my own people again after all these five years. But here we are in Holland. . . ."

"Why yes, that's right," I answered. I was amazed at and impressed by this man who had been under fire and would go under fire again, and was thinking at that moment of things physically so far away; who, in Oosterbeek, remembered Warsaw.

"You see," the man sitting beside me confided, "I was in the defence of Warsaw in 1939. In September. In the first defence. We were holding the Wola sector. One night I went to that little church that's in Wola. You know it, of course. And this church we're in now" —he swept his hand around in a half circle "reminds me of how it was then. Then too there was the glare of fires through the window, only larger fires. And closer. And then too artillery was firing, only heavier. Don't be annoyed if I seem a little sentimental. That was the last night of the defence, and we knew we had got to capitulate. I believed that it was only temporary, that we'd go back. But now, in Holland" he repeated.

Further groups entered the church. It was close on three in the morning. It was time to conduct those who had reached our bank to their positions: We went out. The men fell in irregular, winding lines along the road. We set off.

"Where are our men going?" I asked Captain Zwolanski.

"To the Airlanding Brigade's positions. That's where reinforcements are most needed. I hear that a counter attack is to be made from there tomorrow, as the Germans are too close already."[9]

---

corner embroidered in silver was the Polish diving eagle paratroopers' badge.

In a secret ceremony on 3rd November 1942 the standard was consecrated in the Canon church in Warsaw. After the ceremony the standard was hidden, as there was at that time no way to get it to the men to whom it was dedicated. It remained in Poland until April 1944 when it was smuggled out of Poland by a group of underground leaders into Italy; from here it was flown by Dakota to England. It was presented to Sosabowski by General Sosnkowski on 29th April.

9 It is thought this comment relates to the group of Poles that crossed on the night of 22nd/23rd September and were mainly from the 3rd Battalion. It is said they were met by Lieutenant B. Bottomly (perhaps in the text named as 'Maclean') of the G.P.R., who led them to Divisional H.Q. They were sent to positions on the front line in Stationsweg, relieving a platoon of the 21st Independent Parachute Company. Lieutenant Bottomly was the Intelligence Officer of No 1 Wing.

"More Flying Bombs over London"

"Only some sixty Poles managed to cross to our side last night," Maclean said in the hotel cellar on Saturday morning. "The dinghies went backward and forward, but a dinghy isn't a troop-carrier."

"Sixty or so men won't make much difference to the situation. Perhaps more will be able to cross tonight."

"Possibly," Maclean agreed.

It was really a matter of holding out for how long: twelve, fourteen hours? If during those twelve hours or so the Germans did not open a big attack, and confined themselves to local activities, and of course to artillery and mortars, it would be possible to hold out. Especially as we were getting used to the fire.

I met Alan Wood, and asked him what he thought of the situation.

"It's serious," he answered laconically.

"But how about the Second Army? It's almost reached the other bank."

"I know, but we must remember the river. That's a pretty stiff obstacle."

A little later I went along to the Airlanding Brigade "for breakfast." Of course, I wouldn't get even a smell of breakfast there. I did think I'd get something to eat from my friends who had come across the river, but they, too, had nothing.

"Who wants to eat under such fire?" they muttered morosely. They did not seem at all pleased with their situation.

"How do you feel here?" I asked one of the Polish officers who had come across from the other bank.

"Not too good! As parachutists we're not fond of sitting in trenches," he answered, pulling a face.

"And how are things across the river?" I asked.

"Well, both good and bad. For instance, General Sosabowski charged the German positions on a bicycle yesterday."

"He did what?"

"What I said! Quite unexpectedly yesterday afternoon two British tanks reached us. They had come on rather too fast and had got cut off from the rest. As soon as Sosabowski saw them he was delighted and told them: "Attack those houses in front. Turn the Germans out of them." To which the tank commander replied: "Very good, sir but there are mines there. Someone must lead the way." There was no one available near the house in which the Brigade Command had its headquarters. Everybody was in the fight. But a lady's junior bicycle was standing by the wall.[1] The General got on the cycle and shouted to the tanks:

"Follow me!"

"And what happened?"

"They turned out the Germans. But I've got other news which is very sad. Did you know Tice? "

"2nd Lieutenant Richard Tice? Your volunteer from the United States? Of course, I did."[2]

"He's dead. He died leading his platoon into the attack. We're awfully cut up about it. He'd been in our brigade for several years. He joined the Polish Army when the United States were still neutral."

About midday I set off to go back to the hotel. A very heavy rain was falling, and the artillery and mortar orchestras were at it again. I hesitated whether to jump out of the trench, but it was so cold and damp in this Dutch earth that whatever happened I had to go.

"At the worst I'll only get still more wet."

Though it was broad daylight, I got lost in the forest which I now knew so well. The grey curtain of rain reduced my field of vision. There were no tracks, for they were dug across and along by trenches; the men were shifting their defensive positions deeper into the trees. The trees overthrown by artillery fire lay like beetroots or potatoes torn up in the field.

At first I did not recognise our hotel. I was even inclined to think that at

1 It is recorded that the first link-up by armoured units of XXX Corps and the P.P.B. occurred on Friday 22nd September, when three Daimler Dingo scout cars from the Household Cavalry under the command of Lieutenant R. Wrottesley slipped through the country lanes and made it to Driel. Later that day a small number of Sherman tanks from the 4th/7th Royal Dragoon Guards and some infantry from the 5th Duke of Cornwall's Light Infantry in Bren gun carriers also made it to Driel. Whilst it fair to say that a link-up between the ground forces and the airborne troops was almost within grasp, the troops at Driel were at the end of a long and tenuous corridor that could easily be cut and was hard to defend.

2 Second Lieutenant R. Tice was an American citizen who had no family connection with Poland, but had travelled from the U.S. to England to join the Free Polish Army because of his admiration for Poles who had fought on the U.S. side during the War of Independence. He learnt Polish, refused to transfer to American forces when they entered the war and volunteered for the parachute arm. He passed selection and joined as a trooper, although he was later commissioned. It is reported that when Germans approached his platoon's position, they called out 'Don't shoot', pretending to be friendly forces. The Germans then opened fire and Tice was hit and killed. He now lies in Arnhem Oosterbeek War cemetery, grave 34A13 and was aged 22.

least I had come on it from the wrong side. But there it stood. And I halted before the main entrance. Only the trees which had surrounded the hotel were gone. Gone, too, was the characteristic flowerbed with the pseudo-artistic sculpture in the middle. The white walls of the house were covered with a fine and plentiful riddle of holes from bullets and shrapnel. Instead of windows there were great dark openings without glass, without frames, mutilated by accurate shellfire.

In the afternoon the snipers had their turn again. For at least two hours they terrorised the hotel, the entrance and the neighbouring trenches. The men in the trenches fought back magnificently, against the well-concealed and camouflaged enemy. But their efforts were all but hopeless. The enemy could see them. They could not see him. He was seated in trees and aiming as though on a rifle-range, but they had to search for him. They had to watch, to calculate where he was, and to move as little as possible, and to show themselves still less. Yet two of the less skilful snipers were brought down, like two large pears from the trees.

The "Red Devils" were now as savage as any real devils. They organised volunteer "punitive expeditions" and crept up from different sides towards the spot where a sniper was still firing.

Meanwhile, Dakotas flew over with supplies. The artillery stopped riding over us and turned all its energy to the aeroplanes. Parachutes with baskets sprinkled down over the trees and the trenches, and the men poured out. They knew that sometimes a basket falls into a trench. And then it is better to be outside. Altogether there was quite a lot of confusion.

The "punitive expeditions" took advantage of this diversion to work with extraordinary energy. The snipers were probably momentarily bewildered, and they must not be given time to recover themselves. Several soldiers crawled in a great arc under a tree in which a German was seated. Shots from Sten guns and rifles sped up into the tree, and suddenly the sniper stopped firing. Stopped firing, but started shouting. Probably he wanted to surrender.

Yes, that was it. A youngster, nineteen at the most, slipped down from the tree and raised his hands. He was obviously terrified. His tin hat had fallen from his head, revealing his dark hair, sticky with sweat. Sweat and blood was flowing down his face. Wounded? No, he had only scratched himself on a branch.

The "punitive expedition" took him and led him to the prisoners of war camp. We were surrounded, but our prisoners of war camp still existed.

As a European I was rather edified by this. But as a man whose life had been decidedly embittered by snipers' activities during the past two days, not so much. I went off to my friends' trench, to relieve my feelings to them, and perhaps ... perhaps they had something to eat.

"Please yourself," Johnny Cotterill said. "Either we respect the international conventions, or we don't."

"But the snipers don't respect any conventions," I said. "They aren't always even in uniform. Often they're wearing civilian clothes. And besides ... ."

I stopped, for I saw a *Daily Express* lying at the bottom of the trench. Yesterday's date: Friday, September 22nd. How had it got here? From an aeroplane. A number of copies had been dropped with the supplies.

I forgot that I was hungry, that I was being fired at; I felt a hunger even sharper than physical hunger, a thirst, a need for news.

On the first page, in the second main heading I read:

"More flying bombs over London" The news silenced the shells flying over our heads. I forgot Hartenstein; I forgot our situation, the very uncertain, if not tragic morrow. My wife was in London.

"Have you read about the flying bombs over London?" asked Futer. "My family is there."

"And my wife and children," added a warrant officer from the staff, who had dropped into the trench for a moment, just as I had.

"Is it true that more bombs have fallen on London?" various men asked me in various places during that afternoon.

Those several dozen copies of the *Daily Express* had distracted many of us from our situation, or to the existing anxieties had added another, perhaps the worst anxiety of all for a soldier at the front: anxiety for his family and the safety of those he loves.

"Cuba" and "Roger" do not answer

A storm came on early in the evening. The rain fell spasmodically and lightning flashed almost continually. The German artillery also fired spasmodically, seeming to shake with its own roar and its own malice. The mortars were now firing from very close to us. So close that at times their fire was shifted to points beyond our positions. That evening the acoustics were astonishing and dramatic in their effects. It became difficult to distinguish the type of shot, its origin, and where it exploded. We didn't know whether the roar we had just heard was caused by lightning striking a tree, or by a shell exploding. We didn't know whether the clapping sounds we could hear were made by a German machine-gun or by some new, secret weapon. And we didn't know whose heavy artillery was dropping shells in the immediate proximity of the hotel: ours from the other side of the Lek, or the enemy's. The Germans were so close to us that it was easy to make a mistake; indeed, it was difficult to hit them without doing us injury.

The floor in the dark passage of the cellars was covered with wounded on stretchers. There were many wounded sitting in the large kitchen, too, resting against the stove, the wall, or a box. Wounded men were lying in the small cellarettes in which wine had formerly been stored. And it was from one of these that, as I lit a cigarette and involuntarily threw a light on to my own face, I heard the shout:

"Marek, I'm wounded. Come in with me. Do you know where Johnny is?"

I bent over the man who had called me and recognised him at once. It was Max. A few hours before he had offered me chocolate as he sat in a trench. His ironic face was twisted with a grimace of pain.

"I was transferred to the immediate defence of the house. I sat under the verandah and dug myself into the earth, like the rest. Only to get deeper, deeper," he told me in a husky voice. "And then two tanks suddenly drove along the road. D'you remember those shots which hit the house?"

I certainly did. I was sitting in the signals office at the time, a very reluctantly tolerated guest. I was surrounded with unfriendly glances: I was occupying the precious armchair in which someone else could have been seated; someone else could have been sleeping. Suddenly something began to rattle over the walls of the cellar. Rubble came down and, with it, water. Water in the hotel at Hartenstein! It was almost like a repetition of the miracle worked by Moses in the desert. But it wasn't drinking water. A shell had hit the drainage system, and unpleasant drain water was flooding our cellar.

"That must be an artillery shell," Maclean had declared. It was a shell from a tank gun. The tank crew had fired a lot of shells, and we had a lot of wounded and killed. "I got it in the left arm and leg," Max told me. "The doctor says it's nothing to worry about, it'll heal. But do you know..."

Even in the very poor light given off by two cigarettes smoked close together, I saw a look of terror in Max's eyes. His voice broke and trembled as though that glider pilot was speaking through tears:

"Do you know, I'm being taken prisoner? All the wounded are going to Arnhem. To a German hospital. Our hospital's been smashed, and there's no chance of organising another. Do you know about it? "

Yes, I knew. I had known for some hours past. I knew that we had no chance of looking after and treating our wounded. But could I say so to Max? Confirm the bad news, when he himself did not quite believe it?

"I'll go and look for Johnny," I said, avoiding the unpleasant subject.

Johnny Cotterill was seated in the signals office, voluntarily helping the wireless telegraphist. I told him about Max, and settled down again in the same corner which the tank shells and the leakage in the drainpipe had turned me out of some hours previously.

The room was small, and there were many men in it. Ten perhaps, or even more. They were sitting on a couple of armchairs and chairs, on coal shovelled in one corner, on the cables and wires, and on the floor. Most of them were sleeping.

The telephone exchange was operating in the middle of the room.

"Yes sir," the telephonist on duty answered in a sleepy voice, putting the call through. Sometimes he answered "No sir! No connection now. No, I don't know when, an hour ago there was. They may be cut off. Yes sir, I'll put you through to the chief of staff."

In two opposite corners were two wireless transmitters one English, and one Polish. The British transmitter was taking a rest: it had made contact with the Thirtieth Corps and sent a report. The Polish transmitter was operating in two languages: it was trying to pick up the British "Roger" and the Polish "Cuba "; both of them were operating from the Polish Brigade.

"Hallo Roger, hallo, Roger, here's Seagull. Hallo Roger, hallo, Roger, here is Seagull," Maclean, the volunteer operator, repeated every five minutes or so, in a very weary voice. . No answer. The earpieces quivered with whistles, hisses, jangling, roaring. No human voice answered. "Roger" was silent. "Roger" made no reply.

"Hallo, Cuba, hallo Cuba, this is Roman. Can you hear me? I'm listening. 114110, Cuba, hallo Cuba, this is Roman," the commander of the Polish liaison patrol, Ensign Pajak, patiently repeated in Polish.

No answer, no answer at all. The same hisses, the same whistling and roaring. Like "Roger," "Cuba" made no reply.

"Have you got 'Roger'? " the chief of staff asked, looking in for a moment.[1]

"No sir."

"Have you got 'Cuba?'" he turned to Pajak.

"No sir."

"Go on trying. You must get them," the chief of staff put special emphasis on the "must".

Of course they must. Tonight would be the second night of the crossing. At all costs, at any cost the Brigade must be brought over to our side tonight. During the day several new boats had been built on both sides of the river. Our situation had now ceased to be critical, it was literally tragic. The defenders' forces were melting away. Our ammunition was coming to an end . . . and so were our men.[2]

"Hallo, Roger, hallo Roger … ."

"Hallo, Cuba, hallo Cuba … ."

No answer. Roger and Cuba were both silent.

The door opened violently and General Urquhart walked in. Maclean raised his head and pushed back the earpieces from his ears. The General could read his report in his eyes before he said a word. He put on the earpieces himself.

"Hallo, Roger, hallo Roger, here is Seagull".

Nothing, nothing. Even the General's voice failed to call up the expected signal in the confusion of waves. He tried "Cuba." The same result, damn it!

The General went out; the operators went on torturing themselves.

"Something very strange is happening," Ensign Pajak suddenly remarked in a different tone.

---

1 The Chief of Staff of the 1st Airborne Division was Lieutenant Colonel C. Mackenzie, although his official title was G.S.O. 1 of the Operations Branch.

2 Again I feel Marek may have got confused over the number of 'crossing attempts' and I would ask the reader to refer to Appendix A.

"Are they answering?" Captain Zwolanski raised his head.

"There's an answer, but not from our men." Pajak removed the earpieces, and at once everybody could hear the gutteral, loud call

"Achtung. Achtung. Achtung!"

And then some sentences in German. The Germans were on our line. Someone thought they must be calling on us to stop talking. Someone else expressed the fear that they intended to discover the locality of our station by the use of goniometers, and then they would open up … .

It grew stifling in that little cellar. The air was tense with the mood of a drama which was drawing near to a swift and inevitable end. The house seemed to be rocking with the explosion and blast of bombs. The groans of wounded came in through the thin doors, from the passage. A dozen or more men, strained to their last powers of endurance, weary with lack of sleep, listened to those explosions, heard those groans, and the German *"Achtung."*

I was tired. Three days of starvation, three days without sleep. My head dropped lower and lower, until at last it fell on to the top of the table. I knew nothing more, I heard nothing more. In my drowsy imagination I saw the picture of a garden, very green and sunlit. Plaids were spread under apple trees. I could hear the humming of bees quite clearly. Someone's hand was laid on my head, passed over my face, and I dropped off into a deep sleep. Now there was no Hartenstein, and no green garden. There were no gentle hands. Only complete oblivion and a deep, untroubled sleep.

"We've got to go," Captain Zwolanski tugged at my shoulder. "Time we went."

I awoke. Pajak had at last made contact with the Polish Brigade. The contact was faint and continually interrupted, it broke off and faded out, but it was contact. General Urquhart came – in again. He talked with "Roger." Despite everything, despite all the German efforts the two waves had met. The menacing "Achtung" did not break into the conversation between the Airborne Division and the Polish Brigade. Final decisions had been taken.

Outside the rain had stopped falling. And the German guns had stopped firing. On both sides of our "front" — if what we held and what was around us could be called a "front" at all—activities had ceased. It was close on two in the morning. There was such a total darkness that I had to hold on to Captain Zwolanski's belt in order not, to get lost in this forest, in order to be able to move at all.

We were going to the positions held by the Airlanding Brigade, and then

Five who got away (from right to left) – F/Sgt Williams, Censor; Mr Stanley Maxted, B.B.C. war correspondent; Major Roy Oliver, War Office Publications Officer, who was wounded twice.

This picture was taken in Nijmegen on 26th September in front of a college on Groesbeekseweg, which was being used as a reception centre. From left to right; Sergeant M. Lewis of the A.F.P.U. (this picture was taken with his camera), Squadron Leader H. Coxon of 6080 Light Warning Unit, Major R. Oliver, Stanley Maxted and Flight Lieutenant B. Williams.

to the river bank. We were going? What we were doing could be described in various ways, but hardly by the word "going." We climbed over fallen trees and branches, knocked up against trunks, walked into trees still standing. We fell on to someone's back in a trench, and the "someone " expressed his opinion of us in strong terms. At times it seemed to grow a little lighter, in places where the trees thinned out. At times someone in the darkness asked for a password. A password and reply, which were ironically light-hearted, almost malicious in their frivolity: "Mae West."[3]

3 The passwords for the first few days at Arnhem according to the operational orders were as follows:

- H Hour until 2359 hours D-Day – Challenge Red, Reply Beret.
- 2359 hours D-Day until 2359 hours D+1 – Challenge Uncle, Reply Sam.
- 2359 hours D+1 until 2359 hours D+2 – Challenge Carrier, Reply Pigeon,
- 2359 hours D+2 until 2359 hours D+3 – Challenge Air, Reply Borne.
- 2359 hours D+3 until 2359 hours D+4 – Challenge Robert, Reply Burns.

A group of the British forces who came back from the north bank of the Lower Rhine.

Another shot taken in Nijmegen, this time by Sergeant D. Smith of the A.F.P.U. Just before the evacuation the three A.F.P.U. men and Major Oliver had split the films and photos taken over the previous nine days four ways, so as to try and ensure that at least some material would get back. It shows a group of British forces who came back from the north bank of the Lower Rhine.

We came to a glade, to a road, which should not have been there, and wire, which we had not expected. We had gone astray. We retraced our steps. The soldier we met once more at his post led us through a group of small cottages, across the boards and beams of a shattered shed, to the outposts of

- 2359 hours D+4 until 2359 hours D+5 – Challenge Troop, Reply Carrier.

Only five days' worth of passwords had been thought of and as they had run out impromptu ones had to be thought of. As Marek stated, a challenge of Mae and a reply of West was used on one day.

Some years ago one of the leading lights in the Arnhem Veterans' Club admitted that he had been a member of the R.E.M.E. L.A.D. towards the latter part of the fighting, near the Hartenstein Hotel, when one of the Brigadiers told him off for incorrectly hearing the password. His recollections are that Mae West was used on Sunday 24th September, in which case passwords are still missing for the Saturday and Monday. It is possible that passwords were arranged locally from HQ and have been lost due to the passage of time.

The author of this book after the evacuation.

the Airlanding Brigade. We awoke a sergeant in a trench covered with boards and earth.

"Do you know where your Brigade Command is?" Captain Zwolanski asked.

"Yes, I was there this evening. Not far from where it was yesterday. A hundred yards or so into the forest."

We took a road dividing the forest into two and passed through the gateway of a small villa. The villa had long since been destroyed, but on the gate, as I remembered from visits on previous days, was the name: "St. Peterborough." Yes, in English: "St. Peterborough."[4] We passed the ruins and, relying on our memory, for we could see nothing in that dense thicket, we came upon the large trenches in which the brigade staff had been operating. A hundred yards farther on—they couldn't be far away. Once more we made our way along a road which really didn't exist. Every yard was strewn with trees. We climbed over them with difficulty, very slowly. I went flying on my face more than once.

4 In spite of asking my good friend Geert Maassen from the Gelderland Archives if he knew of a house in Oosterbeek called St Peterborough, we are unable to locate such a place. Our best guess is that Marek meant the Pietersberg house, which was used as a dressing station by 133 Parachute Field Ambulance and is located in Pietersbergseweg in southern Oosterbeek. It is entirely feasible to walk past this house when going from the Hartenstein to the church.

We turned left, then right, and then left again.

The sergeant halted, at a loss.

"Should be here," he said.

We called for the guard. Into the darkness we asked, "Is there anyone here?" Only the silence answered. There was no one.

"It isn't here," we said to the sergeant in an aggrieved tone.

We went on searching. We returned to our starting point, began again, groping through the trees and bushes, over the mounds and ruins. The Brigade Command was completely lost somewhere close to us, lost in an area so small that we could have walked around it in fifteen minutes.

"I don't understand, what's happened?" the sergeant said. "The last few hours of gunfire have completely changed the forest. Or perhaps they've shifted somewhere else."

What was to be done? We could only return to the Divisional Command. But return now – seemed just as impossible. We penetrated deep into the forest, and I began to have reason to fear that if we went on like that we would run into the German positions. In that Egyptian darkness everything and anything was likely. We moved as quietly as we could. We halted behind trees. We planned every few yards, almost every step.

"If only we could have a little light," I muttered.

As though by magic, my wish was at once fulfilled. Light was provided for us by the German artillery, which now brought its well-earned rest to an end. Less than half an hour later we were back at the Divisional Command. We telephoned to the Airlanding Brigade, which sent us a Polish liaison officer, Lieutenant Krysik, to conduct us by way of the Brigade positions to the Lek crossing.[5]

5 2nd Lieutenant A. Krysik was, as Marek stated, a liaison officer who had landed on 17th September as part of the advance party.

We Wait for the Second Army

That second night of the Brigade's crossing brought us still greater fire. A large mill on the river's southern bank was ablaze, and the great wings swung impotently and aimlessly. They had a strange, nightmare appearance, like an apocalyptic cross which now rose high in the air, with arrowing, straddled arms, then dropped to the dark blue line of the forest. Suddenly a crimson flame burst up from the place where the ferry was. Mines? Or the rest of the jetty? Or a rocket burning before it was discharged? From this distance it was impossible to say what was happening.

On the other hand, it wasn't at all difficult to decide that the large group of houses flaming like a bonfire in a south-easterly direction from us was the village of Driel. That was where the Polish Brigade was starting from. And it was coming over to our side. On our side the half circle of the Arnhem suburb was aflame, and the western edge of Oosterbeek was aflame. In other words, the Poles were passing out of one fire into another. From one blaze to another, from one rain of bullets to another.

It was after midnight when to the roar and whistle of the artillery and the whine of mortar shells was added the piercing rattle of machine-guns. But this time it was not simply the tentative raking of the generally quiet "no-man's land" with fire, as it had been yesterday. It was not simply that the Germans were letting us know that they were on the watch and ready. It was firing at a definite target.

The target on the river was clearly to be seen. Several yellow, green and red rockets suddenly coloured the water, dispersing its black shadows. Huddling against the slippery, damp stones of the riverside embankment, we clearly saw a large, clumsy boat break away from the opposite bank and steadily, quite rapidly move in our direction. Above it spread a coloured, flashing irregular umbrella of twinkling points of light. The light shells grew and increased in number, from a small umbrella they enlarged into a great baldachim which hung over the boat throughout its crossing. It shifted with the boat as far as the bank, and as the men climbed out into the thick and sticky mud it passed right over our heads. But the baldachim had to return: another boat was setting out from the southern bank, and after it came another and yet another.

"The whole brigade wants to get across to you today," said the thin officer in command of the group which had just come across. "We shall be with you at last. And to the end. One way or another. . . ."

This officer, Lieutenant Smaczny,[1] could have had no presentiment at that moment that he would indeed remain here to the end. That he would help to cover our retreat during the night of the evacuation. That he would cross the river again, but this time by swimming, for others would already be holding the opposite bank. And that he would not emerge from the river.

The boats crossed the river in zigzag courses. Continually changing course, in order to avoid the German fire. Sometimes it was effectual. Sometimes ...

"My God!" Captain M. said aloud at the sight of a boat which suddenly stood on end and rose out of the water along its entire length. "That's the third."

But we could not stop for regrets or pity at that moment. The reinforcements coming from the other bank must be taken up to their new positions as quickly as possible. That was what they were coming across for. And now time was precious beyond all computation.

Once more we went across the same meadow. Now it was still more brilliantly lighted than it had been yesterday, for the enemy had ranged his mortar fire on it. And machine-guns were raking it. We did not need to move so quietly as on the previous night, for the air was quivering with sound. We ran for a couple of hundred yards bent down, then we crawled across some rise, to find shelter in the thick and high-growing undergrowth of the gardens on the out-skirts of Oosterbeek.

By the church the Poles from the other bank were divided into groups. Some were to go to the Airlanding Brigade, others elsewhere.

"We shall be moving in open file," one of the guides ordered. "There are snipers in the forest, and we may even fall in with a German patrol."

I stood under a large tree and listened to their stories of all the difficulties they had overcome in order to make the crossing. They had tried out rafts, but they had sunk as soon as they were put in the water. They had tried dozens of other ideas, and had even thought of using the doors of the village houses. The sappers had worked right round the clock, and now were under continual fire as they rowed the boats across.[2]

"Nobody could give us a hand, we had to do it all ourselves," Lieutenant

1 Lieutenant A. Smaczny was O.C. of 8th Company of the 3rd Polish Parachute Battalion.

2 No real thought had been given as to bringing boats and efforts to make rafts from trailers and doors were attempted. See Appendix A.

Pudelko remarked with a note of reproach in his voice.[3]

I went off to get some rest in the command of the Divisional Artillery Battery.

"Now things will be better," Johnny Widdicombe welcomed me with a smile. "The Germans are giving us a hell of a time."

At that moment he had no resemblance to the good-looking and well-dressed artillery lieutenant I had known. A long thick growth covered his face; his eyes were red with lack of sleep. It seemed to me that the arrival of the Poles had injected a large dose of optimism into him. And into me, too. Into all of us.

"A hundred already," said Captain Zwolanski, who dropped into the cellar where the Battery Command was at work.

"A hundred and fifty," Lieutenant Pronobis announced at four in the morning.

"Two hundred," someone whispered to me an hour later, at the riverside.

"Well, this time nearly four hundred Poles have got across to us," we heard in the staff on Sunday morning.[4]

That undoubtedly constituted a great success. Though we could not say that the race for time had been won. We were still in an extremely difficult situation. But now at least a part of the mystery was revealed to us, as though in answer to the question how to win that race. The situation appeared to be almost hopeless. The modified and much more modest plans had laid down that the crossing of the Lek was to be covered by forces of the Airborne Division. But it had not been able to cover the crossing. Yet, though the Germans controlled the crossings with their fire, though they held the bridge, the men of the Polish Brigade had got across to us. They had not brought boats with them from England, for as parachutists they could hardly have sapper equipment with them during the action, and could hardly be bothered with boats, especially as they had counted on crossing by the bridge. But their dash, initiative and ingenuity had surmounted all the obstacles.

The situation on Sunday, September 24th, was such as again to inspire us

3 Lieutenant M. Pudelko was 2 i/c of the 3rd Polish Parachute Battalion. He was killed, believed drowned, on the night of 25th/26th September when attempting to swim the Rhine. His body was never found and the Poles do not appear to have any official memorials to the missing but he is nevertheless commemorated on a plaque in Driel which gives the names of all those killed and missing from Operation Market Garden.

4 It would appear that the numbers given here are a little bit over the actual number of men ferried across the Rhine on that night, although accurate numbers are virtually impossible to state.

with optimism. Thrust back from Arnhem, shut in a pocket surrounded by Germans, we still had contact with the outer world. We had fulfilled a large part of our task. With our own strength we had held back the German attack, we had engaged enemy elements in battle, and we had facilitated the Second Army's approach to the Lek. On the other side was the Polish Brigade, which was sending us reinforcements and anti-tank artillery partly, saved from the gliders, as well as infantry; and while holding the southern bank the Brigade would not allow the enemy's choking ring to be closed.

If only the Second Army were to arrive! It would capture Arnhem, and hold the northern bank of the Lek strongly and firmly. But we knew that the Second Army itself had to smash through continual obstacles, and that its advance was being made by continual fighting, and so was bound to be slow. We no longer dreamed of final triumph: the maintenance of our positions. We realised that that was impossible. We wanted only to hold on until the enemy had been driven back from the other side, until our orders and the help of our comrades in arms would enable us to get out of this trap.

"Have we achieved our objectives?" I asked in the Divisional Command.

"In the present conditions undoubtedly," was the answer.

"We must regard our operation as a component part of the action of the 'Allied Air Army.' From the news we have it seems that the action as a whole has had considerable success. That success would have been impossible without the devoted fight of the First Division. If we hadn't held on here and engaged such a large enemy force: two full infantry division, three artillery regiments, and two mortar battalions. All that, against our one division, and, of course, the Polish Brigade."

Before midday the division, reinforced by Polish troops, was to open a counter-attack in all sectors. It would be led by the brigade commander, if he was still alive. If not, by the chief of staff. Or, failing him by a lieutenant. . .

The proportion of officers and other ranks, which had fallen at their posts during the action, was enormous, we learned at the divisional staff. Not one case had been reported of anyone, no matter what his rank or function, no matter what his situation and how fierce the enemy fire, failing to do his duty, and doing it well, precisely, and devotedly.

The Airborne Division was doing far more than it could have been expected to, more than human beings could be called on to do. Though surrounded and cut off, the First Parachute Brigade was taking prisoners, and with the remnants of its strength had attacked the Germans and driven them back.

Only a few officers and a few dozen men were left of the Fourth Brigade. The Airlanding Brigade had recaptured the positions lost to the enemy the previous day.

Sunday was a cloudy and misty day, but the rain had stopped. The monotonous roar continued through the minutes and the hours. We had grown used to it now, and even familiar with it. We only involuntarily quivered at the sound of a burst of machine-gun fire. That meant the enemy had managed to break through again somewhere, or a group had left the Divisional Command trenches to engage in a desperate hand to hand struggle among the shattered trees of the forest. Those struggles were the most embittered of all, and the siege of the Divisional Command was perhaps the most devilish of all.

On the other side were rested and fanatical men. Usually S.S. men, for they formed the advance guard of every German attack. On our side emaciated and hungry men came out of the trenches. Wet through with the rain, covered with mud, trembling with cold and lack of sleep. Worn out by days and nights of fire, to which there was no break or end. Men who continually saw their comrades dying, who carried away the wounded and slowly began to doubt everything, for in these conditions it was impossible not to doubt.

"There aren't any Red Devils any more, there are only dead men waiting to be finished off," the German wireless propaganda proclaimed triumphantly.

No more "Red Devils"?

A group of our men went skirmishing into the forest. They staggered as they went. The enemy Spandau barked ominously. There was a clapping sound in the air. The mortar shells dropped along yard after yard.

Hands scratched with stones and roots, black with dirt, convulsively clutched their Sten guns. Beneath the tin hats eyes glittered with effort and determination.

"They shall not pass!" the Red Devils said to themselves.

And nor did they, the Germans did not pass. The fresh, fanatical S.S. men bent down and withdrew before the fury of the British counter-attack.

"There are 'Red Devils' still. And they're fighting with all their strength."

In the afternoon I managed to pay my usual visit to "my" trench. The sky was clearing a little, and the sun might even come out. We talked a lot about the Second Army, and still more about the baths in Arnhem. Would there be enough baths for all of us? For when the Second Army arrived we would at once take Arnhem and have a bath. In hot water! With soap!

Our dreams of future triumphs were disturbed by the roar of engines.

Aeroplanes coming over. Possibly Dakotas, possibly Thunderbolts, or possibly... We lifted our heads cautiously above the level of the trench.

"Ours or German?" I asked, for I had lost my sense of bearing.

"Our ... Messerschmitts!" Futer tried to joke.

This was the eighth, or the tenth time, I mentally reckoned. The Messerschmitts were showing particular solicitude for the area of the Divisional Command. They flew over two or three times a day and opened up with bursts of fire among the trees. Just as they did now: long bursts of fire went rattling over our heads, ricocheting with a whistle. Shouts arose from the trenches. Psychologically the Messerschmitts' activities were not as important as that of the artillery and mortar fire. But in fact they inflicted serious causalities.

"Where's the Luftwaffe? They never attempt to show themselves," one of my colleagues on a London paper had repeated again and again in talks and articles during the past month.

"Does the Luftwaffe still exist?" we had read the titles of optimistic articles in various newspapers in various languages. Their writers had most of them reached the conclusion that in fact the Luftwaffe no longer existed.

Ah, how gladly I would have seated them beside me in that trench! With what pleasure I would have seen their heads huddled between their knees, to be lifted from time to time with the question

"Is it all over? Are there any more?"

In the hotel cellar I found more Poles. One of them told me of the fight waged by our Polish Brigade on the other side of the river.

"No harm will come to them, they're trading in live commodities," he said.

"What do you mean?" I asked.

"Why, they're trading in slaves. For instance, they took a dozen or more Germans prisoner. Men who had fired at them from the ground as they were landing and a few others. But what can you do with prisoners in such a mobile and extraordinary action? So they appointed Lieutenant Dyrda to lead the prisoners to some Second Army patrol. The lad went off, looking for the patrol, getting lost, cursing his job, the situation, and most of all the Germans. Finally he found a British commander. "I've brought you some prisoners." And the commander asked in amazement: "What, prisoners? Alive?" "Yes." "Really still alive?" "Of course they're still alive." Now Dyrda began to be surprised at their surprise, and to safeguard himself, to avoid further questions he asked the officer to give him a receipt for his cargo. For he thought someone still higher up wouldn't believe he had brought in his prisoners alive. Afterwards he explained that before the war he had been on the reserve, and engaged in business, and that was why he insisted on a receipt.

There were a number of Poles among the wounded that day. One sergeant didn't want to hand over his weapons to the medical orderly.

"How can I be left without anything in the war?" he explained to me. "Tell that joker for me that there are Germans all around."

It wasn't necessary to explain that to the "joker," but the orderly was not to be moved. The wounded were going to the Red Cross hospital. They couldn't take any weapons with them.

"There's a Pole lying out in the passage asking to speak to one of his own people," Bruce Davis told me.

The Pole, lying on a stretcher, was a rifleman, Victor Chmielewski.[5] He had been struck by mortar shrapnel in the backbone. "My hands," he said. "Put my hands better, for I can't move them, and they're not properly arranged. And some water."

I adjusted his hands; at each movement he grimaced with pain. His young, immature face was twisted with the pain of his suffering; his words came to his lips with great effort, and were distorted, difficult to understand.

I asked the doctor what would happen to this man. He replied with a very mournful smile and a gesture of resignation.

"Tell me, have I got to die? I'm only twenty," Chmielowski whispered.

"You won't die. It's nothing," I comforted him.

"You see, if I died, or if I was left a cripple, without arms, or without legs . . . you see, I'm hit in the loins … You know … Write down that I'm from Vilno. And that I spent two years in Russia … In the north. But now I'm fighting. In Holland. And that I came here in order to return to Vilno. You see, I come from Vilno. Write that in your articles."

Someone touched my shoulder.

"I've just come back from a funeral," Lieutenant Pronobis told me with a wry twist of the lips. "We've filled in the trench of Captain Glazurek[6] and some others of our lads. Lieutenant Kutrzeba's dead, too, killed when he went … ."

5 Private V. Chmielewski is believed to have been a member of the Anti-Tank Battery and his date of death is given as 22nd September 1944. He has no known grave.

6 Captain I. Glazurek's date of death is given as 24th September; he was O.C. 9th Company of the 3rd Parachute Battalion. His field burial was in the garden of 8 Stationsweg, close to the crossroads in Oosterbeek, which was a hotly contested area on the eastern part of the perimeter. It was to houses on this road that he and his men were sent after crossing the river probably in the early hours of the Saturday. He now lies in the Arnhem Oosterbeek War cemetery grave 25B5 he was aged 37.

But he had no time to tell how Lieutenant Kutrzeba met his death.[7] A Spandau began to bark away somewhere quite close. The bullets struck against the wall of the hotel, sprinkled through the remnants of the windows and over the still remaining glass of the vestibule roof. Several men ran down from upstairs with a muffled clatter. It was the patrol which had been in the hall.

"What are you doing here?" asked a warrant officer, the commander of the staff defence. He was a tall dark English-man with large moustaches, with a piece of ordinary white rope round his waist in lieu of a belt, and a revolver without holster thrust behind the rope. The warrant officer acted as a kind of traffic control in the cellar, receiving wounded from the trenches, sending them off in wagons to hospital, and above all seeing that there were not too many men crowding the narrow passages of the cellar.

"What are you doing here?" he said to the patrol. Pointing to the stairs, he added: "Go back where you came from."

The men went back, but at that moment there were several further bursts from the Spandau.

"There's a sniper letting fly up there, sir. Straight at us," one of the patrols explained in an apologetic tone.

"We can't see him, but he's got us on a plate," another added.

"A sniper?" the warrant officer shrugged his shoulders. D'you know what snipers are for? For you to finish off. Up you go!"

"Yes sir," they answered, and obediently went upstairs.

Discipline was still irreproachable. And because of that circumstance the entire division was carrying on as though at exercises. And because of it the troublesome sniper also shared the fate of his predecessors, a few minutes later.

So another night slowly came on at Hartenstein. Sunday night, a night as ill-boding, as noisy with shells, as ominous with expectation.

The fire burns merrily in my London flat as I try to recall all the details of the last night we spent in that hotel. But the details fade, are mixed inextricably, are covered with a kind of mist, or veil. I cannot distinguish the hours and I have no idea how time passed. Time had ceased to exist, or in any case had ceased to be reckoned. And steadily the fates grew fewer and the incidents fewer, too.

7 Lieutenant J. Kutrzeba was O.C. of the Mortar Platoon of the 3rd Parachute Battalion, he was also killed on 24th September and it is believed he was first buried in the Hemelseberg area, which is to the south-west of the Hartenstein. He now lies in the Arnhem Oosterbeek C.W.G.C cemetery grave 25B6 and was aged 32.

"Well, what happened that night?" my wife asked me, as I dictated my story of Arnhem to her.

"I don't know, I don't remember … "

I took out my notebook in which I had written my dispatches and kept a diary. Unfortunately, I cannot read most of what I had written, for during the night of evacuation across the Lek the notebook had a bath, and the water washed away many memories and thoughts. But a few of those pages were saved. For instance, the beginning of a dispatch sent on Monday, a strange, peculiar dispatch which I knew I would not be able to send away, because by then our wireless transmitter had ceased to function. This is what I wrote:

"The night of September 24th. Somewhere near Arnhem. Everything would seem to point to our situation having become tragic. We are held in an arc of which the chord is the River Lek. Our only hope of help is from the other side of the river. The German artillery and mortars are going it for all they're worth. At times the fire is impossible to endure. The forest around our positions has to a large extent been felled by shells. We're waiting for the Second Army."

And a little farther on is a personal reflection:

"I don't know which is worse: lack of sleep or hunger. At times it seems to me that I'm very hungry and I justify my laziness by that fact. I've not been anywhere today, because I feel rather weak. At times I am possessed with a yearning for a few hours free of this roar. If only I could have a good sleep."

"I'm curious to see how all this will end. We were told today that the Second Army is several miles from the other side of the river. But will it be able to cross? We know from the experience of the Polish Brigade how difficult that is. And yet that was a question of bringing only a few people across. Now it would be a matter of equipment, tanks, and guns. If they don't get across to us by tomorrow (or yet perhaps the day after tomorrow) it's all up. Or imprisonment in the best case. To be taken prisoner in the sixth year of the war, when we're beating the Germans on every front … I am coming to the conclusion that I'm a particularly inefficient war correspondent."

"The staff is operating continuously, and General Urquhart is irreproachably undisturbed. He even shaves every day, though he uses a dry razor, for we haven't had any water for a long time. His calm and cheeriness are really the sole source of our optimism. I believe that man will manage to handle the situation."

"The signals office is extraordinarily active. I hope something will come of it. Something must come of it. Today we picked up a bit of the B.B.C.

news. The Second Army is nearing Arnhem. They all realise our situation. It is impossible that we should be left to our own bitter fate."

Death on the Rhine

"It's going to be fine," Bruce Davis said with a solemn face on Monday morning, September 25th.

Bruce Davis is an optimist, and a friend of mine. As an optimist he had been declaring for a day or two past that the Second Army was some three miles away. As my friend he had brought me exultantly a single biscuit from an American field ration.

"The last!" he clapped me on the back. His smile was rather like that of a child. "When it's gone we'll starve! Shan't we, Mark?"

"We shall!" I answered with gratitude, and, without knowing why, I stretched out my hand to his.

I thought Bruce was right: the German guns and mortars had definitely died down, and only two or at the most three batteries were troubling about us. It was almost quiet, and for the first time for a long period I took the tin hat off my head. I felt definite relief, and recalled that I hadn't undressed, or washed, or shaved for six days. We all had thick growths of hair, and Bruce with his beard looked like an old, bearded monk.

"There are a few cigarettes for the wounded. Only for the wounded," said the medical orderly. "Half a cigarette for each man."

Hands were stretched out eagerly from the floor and the few chairs, from mattresses and stretchers. In one corner of the kitchen, which had been turned into a hospital ward, a Polish corporal sat next to a German S.S. man, a sniper who had been taken prisoner. The corporal had his left leg bandaged; the S.S. man was wounded in the neck and hand.

"For you and him," the orderly said to the Pole, pointing to the German.

The corporal lit the cigarette and drew at it slowly, carefully, with long pulls, enjoying the flavour of the tobacco and the scent of tobacco smoke. When only half was left he nudged the German with his elbow.

"Cigarette?"

"*Danke*," the German muttered and greedily took the cigarette.

"If anyone had ever told me I'd give a rotter from the. S.S. a cigarette, I wouldn't have believed him. What an idiotic war!" The corporal complained to his comrades.

The war certainly was "idiotic," for now the German fire suddenly ceased entirely. At once the rumour began to run through the hotel cellars that we had capitulated. In an hour, the general story ran, the Germans would be arriving and we would be laying down our arms. I went to the staff to find out the truth. All nonsense, of course. No one was capitulating, we were going on fighting. But during the night we should all be evacuating to the southern bank of the river. All, that is, who could move. And the wounded? The wounded would remain behind.

As it was quiet, I decided to run to the jeep in which we had left our rucksacks. A small fortune was in them, two 24-hour food rations, a thousand cigarettes, and my pullover, hand-made by my wife. The jeep was not far off, barely twenty, or maybe thirty yards from the house, but for several days the German fire had been coming steadily in that direction. I had tried several times before, always without success. And now, hardly had I stepped outside the hotel when the fire began again. The glass roof above the verandah crashed down with a terrifying jangle. I jumped across the remnants of the border, and then squatted down under the remains of the marble sculpture, and at last reached the spot where the jeep had been. For it was there no longer. Large trees cut down by shells had crushed the car into the ground, smashing and squashing it completely. I saw only the pieces of one wheel, a little iron, and blankets. I could not find the rucksacks. I ran back. And the firing ceased.

Punctually at eight in the evening the German symphony of death was struck up again. We soon realised that it was not the usual fire. It now had an unprecedented violence. There were an unprecedented number of guns and mortars. A devilish intensity of fire-power. And . . . heavy artillery!

Now the house shifted as though on wheels. And not only the house: at times it seemed that even the earth was stirring anxiously, that we were in the midst of a revolving stage slowly turning on its centre. It was nine o'clock, and Lieutenant Sawicki said that he must go to find his men. He had come to the staff simply to get further orders.[1]

"How far are they?" I asked.

"Well, at least a hundred yards."

A hundred yards! In the existing conditions that was an enormous distance. A hundred yards under fire there, and a hundred yards under fire back.

"Why didn't you bring them earlier?" I asked Sawicki, but he only shrugged

1 Lieutenant S. Sawicki was an Assistant Quartermaster with the 1st Parachute Battalion.

his shoulders

"Who would have been left to hold the positions?"

"All right then, off you go," I said in a resigned tone. He went out; but he came back at once.

"It's quite impossible," he declared. "Shells are falling one after another. A fly couldn't get through."

After several minutes he tried again. And returned again. "Somebody will get your men out of the trench," I said. "They're all going."

"But they're waiting for me; I said I'd go back," he answered.

In the end he decided to chance it, whatever happened. I met him and his men next day at Nijmegen.

General Urquhart, Colonel Preston and several other staff officers came out from the commander's office. They were calm, and carried canes. A young lieutenant with sad eyes and a melancholy smile on his face, in his shirt sleeves, his shirt dirty and sweaty, leaned against the door frame. The divisional doctor.

He was remaining behind, for the wounded were remaining. In a few hours he would be a prisoner, with his patients. General Urquhart went up to him and took his hand "Goodbye, doctor."

"Goodbye, sir."

The General saluted. We others stood to attention.

At 10.45 we too slipped out of the hotel in the forest.

We were struck by a glaring, terrifying, crimson light. Everything all around us was on fire. The neighbouring villages were blazing, the forest was blazing. Over our heads mortar shells burst, scattering thousands of pieces of shrapnel around us. The air was vibrating with the whistle and, hiss of artillery shells. The fallen trees made our way difficult, branches entangled our feet, deep craters forced us to change our direction every minute or two, or to leap across and go round the road of our retreat.

We plunged into a shallow depression and could not stir a yard in any direction. We were framed by arrowing explosions, repeated with terrifying monotony always in the same spots. Our guide went on ahead, but a moment later he fell to the bottom of the hole, struck by shrapnel. Someone else took over the lead, but he shared his predecessor's fate.

"Should we stay there longer, or go on?" we all asked ourselves. Each could answer as he wished.

We jumped out in two's and three's and flew straight towards the ring of fire. We were driven on by blind instinct, not by prudence, not by foresight, nor by calculation. Another step, a couple of steps, and the spectral frame of fire was behind us.

After going on for some dozens of yards I ran into another group, then another and another. All the retreating force was split up into groups, which melted into one another, mingled and then separated again. I lost my own group at a turn in the path. I attached myself to another, only to lose that too, through taking shelter behind some bushes. I knew that whatever might be happening in front, whatever the strength of the barrier, which the enemy might raise before us, I could not lie down. I could not remain still! For a moment I recalled that the Poles with men of the Dorsetshire Regiment, sent across to our side of the river the previous day, were covering our retreat. That they must be lying down under still heavier fire, were waiting. And that must be horribly unpleasant.[2]

Then I ran on again.

Now there was no one in front of me, so I halted. But I was wrong. Several men extended under fallen trees were waiting for the fire before us to slacken a little. I lay down behind the last man, but the group went on waiting and waiting. Others passed us, others ran through, but these went on lying. So I caught hold of the soldier next to me by the shoulder:

"Get up, get up!" I shouted.

But he slipped stiffly through my fingers. The man in front of him was the same. These men would never get up. The trees beneath which they had fallen marked the last bound of their journeying.

I flew past a crossroads, then the burning houses of Oosterbeek. Now I was in the meadow, I rolled like a ball down a slope, the mud squelched in my boots, mud flowed down my face, mud mixed with sweat and blood. Not my blood, but of those I had tried to raise from the dead.

Men were lying and cows were running on the very edge of the river. The cows were terrified. They galloped about in herds, fell on the men, fought

2 The evacuation of the 1st Airborne Division (or what was left of it and able to walk) took place on the night of 25th/26th September and was called Operation Berlin. When a student at the Staff College pre-war Major-General Urquhart had studied the evacuation from Gallipoli in Turkey at the end of a somewhat disastrous campaign in 1915 and 1916, and he based his plan for evacuation on techniques used there. This consisted of a collapsing bag principle with those at the northern part of the perimeter leaving first. To guide men to the two crossing points glider pilots and engineers were used to mark the route with white tape and to stand at strategic locations as human marker posts. Men left in small groups under a heavy barrage from the guns of XXX Corps some miles to the south. It also helped that it was raining and the men had done their best to muffle their boots by wrapping things such as lengths of curtain material round them.

among themselves.

And over the river flew machine-gun fire. Light shells of crimson, violet, yellow and blue. A bouquet of such lights came flying in our direction. I fell on the ground and searched for something under which to take cover. Someone's hand stretched out to me from beneath a dead cow. A hand seized me firmly by my overall and dragged me closer.

"There's room for us both, friend," someone whispered.

I crawled under the cow, huddled against the dark form and lay still for several seconds, or maybe minutes, which seemed years.

"But how your heart's beating," my friendly neighbour remarked. "You shouldn't get too worked up." Involuntarily I smiled.

A burst of machine-gun fire came together in a bouquet, and something caught alight in the middle of the river. Probably a boat hit by accurate mortar fire. Right above us things had quietened down a little, so we ran along the bank. Hundreds of men were squatting in the mud, and more men were arriving all the time. But the Germans now shifted their fire from the forest from the road, from Oosterbeek, and dropped it on the bank. The shells tore into the grey, huddled mass of men, and there was no shelter from them.

One could only have faith in one's destiny, in one's luck.

"The trajectory of a shell takes the form of a parabola," I recalled scraps of definitions. At that moment I could see thousands of light shells describing regular parabolas. One could tell in advance where each of those shells would fall. Death was flying above us, and we saw that death. It was as colourful as the picture of some fantastic legend, as some Disney Silly Symphony. And because of its colour, because of the multitude of tints, because of the roar and the hiss and the whistle, this death was unusually menacing: for it deprived one of strength before it killed, it paralysed before it arrived.

Every few dozen yards glider pilots stood on the bank. Our "iron guard." They directed the crowd of men, allocated groups to the approaching boats, mentally registered further groups as they came up.

"Here's the queue," a stocky, ginger-whiskered captain standing in front of us said in a very quiet, steady voice, and he pointed to a small sector of the bank, only a few yards long.

"That man's like a bobby in the middle of Oxford Circus," I thought.

"Don't panic, don't panic!" the captain repeated incessantly.

But there wasn't any sign of panic, only perfect order. Irreproachable discipline. At every step there was exemplary, touching brotherhood. The evacuation was proceeding according to plan.

When my turn came I waded up to my waist through the water, climbed into the boat, seized an oar, and rowed. For a moment I had a delusory feeling of security, but then the fire again shifted to fly over our heads, to hunt and pursue us, until right under the opposite, the safe southern bank of the river a solid fragment tore into the back of the boat. We fell out, swam a couple of yards and then, at last … .

At last? Well, not quite. When I crawled up the riverside embankment on that farther side I realised that here, too, shells were falling. Far, fewer, truly… But here they came!

It was raining (though it might have been raining all the time, and I simply hadn't noticed it). The road was narrow, filled with holes and craters. A short, sturdy British soldier briskly stamped along with his muddy boots clattering on the pitted asphalt. I could not see his face, but I recognised his voice. Not so much recognised it, as tried to recall where I had heard it before. Ah, now I remembered. It was he who had dragged me under the dead cow. And he had said that my heart was beating hard.

"Thank you," I said to him. "What's your name?"

"Martin. I'm a Scotsman, from Perth. What's yours?

"I'm a Polish war correspondent, but I don't suppose you could pronounce my name."

"Fine! So you must know Scotland."

"Of course I do."

"Ever been in Perth?

"Yes."

"And in Edinburgh, Aberdeen, Falkirk, Cupar?"

We walked farther and farther away from Arnhem and we talked continually about Scotland.

Outside a large shed, perhaps two miles or more from the river, we were given hot tea, sandwiches and rum. We were given more hot tea near Nijmegen. We were wrapped in military blankets and packed in twenties and thirties into large American lorries. The end of the journey promised to be entirely pleasant.

"Now at any rate we can travel without adventure," I said boastfully, as I made myself comfortable in one corner of the lorry.

"Cross your fingers," my neighbour said in a tired voice.

He was right. It was certainly very wise to cross one's fingers, or to touch wood. Especially in this case, for after travelling a couple of hundred yards the lorry overturned at a bend in the road. For a moment the men lay in a heap, not moving and not uttering a word.

"Don't panic, don't panic!" someone mimicked the warning we had heard so often during the evacuation.

There was a roar of laughter. We all laughed louder and louder, more and more happily, more and more carefree. For what was this stupid accident compared with the night we had just come through?

"To Arnhem"

"After eight hours the last boat was sent to the bottom," I was told by a corporal of the Airborne Division, whom I met next afternoon in the streets of Nijmegen. "German tanks opened fire from behind a hedge. What could we do? Several of us flung ourselves into the water to swim across. Poles were swimming at my side. There was a Polish officer among them. He didn't get across ... "[1]

I know that officer was either Lieutenant Smaczny or Lieutenant Pudelko. Both of them were hit by German bullets while they were in the water, and both met their death in the river.[2]

"How many men got across to our side that way, do you think? I asked the corporal.

"I don't know, but I think quite a lot. I hope more will still turn up."

The anaemic afternoon sun was warming the streets of Nijmegen; the houses had black gaping holes in lieu of windows. Our muddy uniforms, wet socks, and boots with legs pulled absurdly high were heavy and chilled us through. We were seated in the mess of one of the British units, surrounded

---

1 Two crossing points had been nominated, but in spite of some communication between those on the south bank with those on the north, the plan made did not conform to the actual conditions on the north bank. Urquhart's plan for the withdrawal of those men north of the Rhine was fine but it was assumed at 43rd Division H.Q. that the attempts to move men across on the previous night had been successful and had widened the perimeter. This meant that two points were nominated to evacuate from, one near the ferry point where men had been landed the previous night and one near the artillery positions by the church in southern Oosterbeek. Urquhart knew nothing of this and intended to send all his men to the point near the church. Two routes to here had been marked out, one passing each side of the Hartenstein.

Each of the crossing points had been allocated two engineer companies, one from the 43rd Division with assault crafts which had no other power except that of the men inside and a company of Canadian engineers with 'storm boats' powered by outboard motors. The Canadian boats could do the trip in about three minutes; it obviously took longer for the British boats to paddle across. It is believed the Canadians made 150 trips during the night – attempts to keep an accurate count failed because the paper turned to pulp in the downfall. However, it is fair to say that they carried the majority of the men across. The engineer companies involved were 260 and 533 Field Companies, 20 and 23 Canadian Field Companies.

The official tally of men who crossed the river was 2,398 – 1st Airborne Division including glider pilots, 2,163; Poles 160 and 4th Dorsets 75. However, if one adds together individual unit returns the total is about 2,500. It is said about 100 Poles were left behind on the north side of the river, but this does include wounded men who were unable to leave the dressing stations.

2 It is fairly easy to confirm that the officer lost was Lieutenant Pudelko as Lieutenant Smaczny (O.C. 8th Company 3rd Parachute Battalion) survived the battle.

by officers with neatly pressed battledress and irreproachably polished boots. Glasses of rum, whiskey, gin and beer were standing on the table. We told the epic of Arnhem. We were proud of the mud on our uniforms, of the tin hats on our heads, of our dirt and our past. A tall, thin brigadier came up to us, and once more we told the story from the beginning. Dusk fell, it grew darker in the room, the minutes and the hours passed.

"To Arnhem!" Someone proposed the toast.

"To the Red Devils!" I added.

A British officer who happened to pass through the room at the moment came up to me. He rested his hand on my shoulder and said in a tone which expressed a certain amazement and admiration

"Another Pole turned up a few minutes ago. He had hidden almost all day in the bushes, and managed to swim across the Lek only this afternoon."

"You were talking of the 'Red Devils' one of the British officers remarked. "You proposed a toast in their honour. I'd like to take it up and add to it: "To the Red Devils and their Polish comrades."

Through the window we saw the brilliant light of searchlights sweeping the sky. In the distance we heard the roar of aeroplanes.

"They're our … Messerschmitts," I repeated the joke made in the trench at Hartenstein.

Artillery opened fire from the ground. This time it was our artillery. Allied artillery. We knew that it would advance, and that the tanks and infantry would advance to Arnhem. Perhaps tomorrow, perhaps in a week, or maybe in a month. But they would get there for certain.

They would sweep on to complete the task the 'Red Devils' had begun.

London, October 24th, 1944.

Appendix A

The attempts to cross the Rhine

As we have seen, the P.P.B. should have dropped onto DZ K, to the south of the Arnhem road bridge, on Tuesday 19th September but as things were not going to plan, this DZ was moved westwards near to a village called Driel almost opposite Oosterbeek, but still on the south side of the Rhine. As it turned out bad weather in England stopped the P.P.B. taking off until Thursday 21st September. Their commander Sosabowski had been told before he took off for Holland to cross the river using the Driel ferry, which was in 'British hands'.

Lieutenant S. Kaczmarek of the Support Echelon commented:

> Sosabowski sent me with Captain Budziszewski, the Engineer Company commander, and fifteen men. It was dark when we reached the ferry site about an hour later. We stood on the ramp, and Captain Budziszewski shouted a big "Hello", but there was no reply from the other side. Then he put up a flare, but as soon as it lit up, there broke out a hell of a fire from the opposite bank. We dashed and took cover behind some heaps of cobblestones and it was a miracle that none of us were hit. The firing went on for about five minutes and we could hear it ricocheting off the stones. We returned to Driel when the firing stopped and reported back. So there was nothing doing that night.

In spite of this one of the Polish liaison officers at the Hartenstein, Captain L. Zwolanski, volunteered to swim across the Rhine with the news that the 1st Airborne would attempt to widen the bridgehead around the Westerbouwing heights and at the same time sappers would prepare some boats to start moving the P.P.B. across near the church in Oosterbeek. The attempt to retake the heights failed and the construction of makeshift boats using trailers was a failure. Other efforts to find boats on the south bank and make rafts out of doors also failed.

Friday 22nd September

Around noon in Oosterbeek, the commander of No 3 Troop from the 4th Parachute Squadron Royal Engineers, Captain Harry Faulkner-Brown, was instructed to report to the Commander R.E. (C.R.E.) Lieutenant Colonel E. Myers at the Hartenstein Hotel. Upon arrival Harry was instructed to take part of his troop, and ferry as many Poles across the river as possible. Let me continue in Harry's own words:

> The C.R.E. further instructed me to collect some two-man inflatable dinghies, called recce boats, from a house at a map reference I cannot now remember but it was south of the Hartenstein and carry out a ferrying operation during the hours of darkness. He hoped it might result in perhaps as many as 200 Polish reinforcements. He told me to make for the church near the river, cross the wide polder due south and head for the river.
>
> In the early afternoon I set out in a jeep to collect the recce boats. I arrived at the house; it was a single storied timber building. I approached it and spoke to the occupants through an open window. There I found Kelly, one of my NCOs, who told me the house was being used as an overflow for the walking and not seriously wounded. I told him the reason for my visit and he limped off to find the only officer there. This was an immaculately dressed padre who was clean-shaved, who looked far different from me. He told me that there were six recce boats and one large R.A.F. dinghy, probably taken from a crashed plane. After I loaded them all on to our jeep he offered me a cup of tea in a fine china cup and saucer. As I was drinking it and he was engaging me in conversation a mortar bomb exploded behind me on the drive and a large splinter whistled past my right ear, passed through the open window and struck the padre leaving a four inch slash across his throat.[1]
>
> I carefully selected the twelve sappers who were to accompany me. We loaded ourselves and our equipment on two jeeps and set off as dusk was falling. As well as the boats, we had tracing tapes, reels of signal cable and a liaison officer with a wireless set connected to Divisional H.Q.

After a few trials and tribulations Harry's party reached the church and then moved across the polder:

1 This was Padre H. Irwin, attached to the 11th Parachute Battalion, who later died of his wounds.

We then came to an anti-flooding dyke about four feet high, on the other side of which we encountered the river. The banks shelved down gradually to the water. Stone groynes projected out to about fifty yards into the water and were spaced at about a hundred yards along the shoreline. They were rather high and gave shelter and slack water from the swiftly flowing current, so that the actual shoreline was ideal for loading and unloading.

My first task was to organise our little beachhead into a defensive position. Then I rowed over the Rhine to make contact with the Poles. I was welcomed on the other side by a group of Poles, some of whom I could just understand. I informed them that I had decided to attach signal cable to each end of the little rubber dinghies and pull them across the river so that we would have boats at six crossing points at which two men at a time would be pulled across the river. The Poles told me that they wanted a Polish liaison officer to go back with me and represent them on the north bank. I then rowed back to the Oosterbeek shore where I was warmly welcomed by my men. They had fears I would not reappear. Signal cable was now attached fore and aft to one recce boat and a sapper with a large reel of cable set off for the other side. Although this was just the beginning I had the feeling that everything was going well. The recce boat was being rowed across the Rhine, it had just got past the end of the stone groyne when the full flow of the current caught it and the cable parted. We tried it again, but without success. I really felt rather upset because I immediately realised that my idea of using cable was a poor engineering decision. Signal cable is of very small gauge, has little tensile strength and this now proved inadequate and frankly naïve. The recce boats would have to be rowed back and forth by my sappers, there could only be one soldier passenger instead of my over-optimistic two.

We had not been rowing very long when Lieutenant David Storrs, the Field Engineer from the C.R.E., joined us. He told me that he had been here the previous night and offered his athletic prowess as a rower. I gave him a recce boat and off he went. By a display of an amazing show of guts, strength and perseverance, he rowed back and forth twenty-three times, delivering one Polish soldier on each trip. My men were tired and hungry before we even started and as the night drew on I was aware that we were not operating at our best. The Polish liaison officer who I had brought over kept complaining to me of the slow progress. I could only agree with him. I detailed L/Corporal Brown, to take the R.A.F. rescue dinghy and a crew of three and load it up with Poles. It was about six feet in diameter and I

> thought with care it could take four passengers. Off they went but as soon as they got into the main current the dinghy became unmanageable and was swept downstream. It was obviously very difficult to control and almost impossible to steer. It was carried some distance downstream before they were able to beach it, but they managed to find their way back.
>
> Our problems were increased when two of the recce boats were punctured and were unusable. The Polish liaison officer was becoming a problem with his continuing critical complaints about our slowness. The rowers were experiencing some difficulties on the far side because some of our Polish comrades could not speak or understand English, they all seemed to be over equipped and some of them rather over excited.

All in all not a good result – Harry felt that only about forty Poles were ferried over in this way. Martin Middlebrook states that fifty-two came across. Perhaps relations were not helped by the continuing complaints on the north bank, about which Harry did something that is not normal behaviour for an officer – "I was not at the end of my tether, but I was very tired and I realised I had to get rid of him. I drew my Browning automatic and quite deliberately pointed it at his belly and said quite quietly; "If you don't f**k off, I'll shoot you." I didn't see him again."

Around 0400 on the Saturday morning the ferrying was stopped, possibly due to German interference and tiredness. It was soon after when Harry was counting heads near the church when he realised he was one man short, L/Corporal Flannery was on the south bank. Fortunately Harry and one sapper were able to row across the river and collect him unscathed.

Saturday 23rd September

At least the failure of the attempt using rubber dinghies identified to senior minds the impracticality of using these craft to reinforce the 1st Airborne Division north of the Rhine. So during the morning Major-General Sosabowski had sent his chief of staff, Major R. Malaszkiewicz, further south to point out the impossibility of using rubber dinghies and to ask for proper assault boats. He reached the H.Q. of the 43rd Division's 130th Brigade and was warmly welcomed by its commander Brigadier B. Walton. Walton said that he had eighteen large boats, each capable of holding twenty four men – the P.P.B. could expect them at 2000 and Canadian sappers attached to the Division would crew them.

Apparently Major Malaszkiewicz did not arrive back in Driel until around 1900, so a quick plan had to be made. Captain Budziszewski's Engineer Company was to be responsible for organising the crossing. Some of the sappers would go with the first wave to provide security on the north bank and hopefully turn the boats round quickly. The plan was that the 3rd Battalion would go first, followed by Brigade H.Q., the 1st Battalion mortar platoon, the admin units and finally the 2nd Battalion. Commanders were advised that the boats would be crewed by the British and to divide their men into groups of eighteen.

The boats did not arrive until just before midnight, there were no boat crews and so men from the Engineer Company had to carry out the task, as another observer has put it, "with unfamiliar equipment, in the dark and under much heavier German fire than on the previous night."

The first crossing did not take place until 0300 on the Sunday morning because of the above problems, and because the boats had to be dragged and carried 500 yards over fields, ditches and a high bank. It is fair to say that what happened that night was to affect the reputation of the Poles and their commander for a long time. Then at the riverside a further problem was met – the boats were found to be only able to take twelve so a further reorganisation was needed and caused much confusion. The engineer commander, Captain Budziszewski, is recorded as "swearing like a Polish officer had never been heard to swear before."

The C.R.E. of the 1st Airborne Division was present on the south bank and commented, "I can find no fault with their attempts; they did as much as they could. They had not been trained in river crossings and the Arnhem plan had not envisaged one and no one had any proper boats. But the less said about their watermanship the better."

Again daylight brought a halt to any further crossings. It is said that 153 men were ferried across; 95 from the 3rd Battalion, 44 anti-tank gunners and 14 from Brigade H.Q. This was less than a quarter of the number hoped for. Sosabowski was not amongst those who crossed and returned back to Driel with the majority of his command.

Sunday 24th September

It was realised that after a week the 1st Airborne Division was in a dangerous position and a major crisis was looming. In the morning the commander of XXX Corps Lieutenant-General Horrocks came up to Driel to see Sosabowski and the situation for himself. They went up the church tower at Driel and Horrocks asked Sosabowski for his opinion as to what should be done. Sosabowski suggested two options; either to make a major reinforcement across the Rhine or withdraw the airborne men before they were totally wiped out. According to the P.P.B. war diary, "Horrocks indicated that he supported the first option; he intended to put a battalion of the 43rd Division with supplies over the river that night close to 1st Airborne's positions and follow with a complete brigade at what was hoped to be an unopposed crossing at Renkum, four miles downstream."

Later that day a conference was convened at Valburg, about halfway between Driel and Nijmegen to which Sosabowski was invited to, to go over the details for that night's attempt. Sosabowski took Lieutenant J. Dyrda with him as he was one of the best English speakers in the Brigade.

At this conference, held in a tent, Sosabowski sat on one side with three British generals (Horrocks, Browning and Thomas commander of the 43rd Division) and their staffs on the other. Dyrda was not even allowed to sit down and had to stand behind his commander. It was certainly not a round-table conference and as Jerzy Dyrda commented it had "the appearance of a court-martial session, where on one side sat the judges and opposite them the accused, alone."

Horrocks, opening the meeting, stated there would be two crossings that night, both under the command of Major-General Thomas, to whom he then handed over to. Giving only the briefest of details, he said that the 4th Dorsets from the 130th Brigade, followed by the 1st Polish Parachute Battalion, would cross close to the site of the Driel ferry and aim to capture the Westerbouwing heights. A second crossing consisting of the rest of the P.P.B. would take place further to the east, on the site of the previous attempts. Both crossings were to start at 2200 and under the overall command of Brigadier Walton. It was later reported that Sosabowski was annoyed and shocked by the way in which one of his units had been taken from him without even the opportunity to nominate the unit, a departure from even the most basic of military political correctness. Lieutenant Dyrda, translating all of this into Polish for Sosabowski, did not pass on the point about a Polish major-general having to give up control of one of his battalions to a young English brigadier who had not even viewed the area of the crossings.

There was then silence. None of the English officers present asked any questions, an indication perhaps that they already knew what was going on.

Sosabowski rose to his feet and via Jerzy Dyrda suggested that the crossing point for the Dorsets and his 1st Battalion would arrive at strong points in the German defences. He added he had been observing German movements and was convinced that a landing further westwards would be unopposed. He sat down. Major-General Thomas did little more than repeat the orders, according to Jerzy Dyrda, "very surely and unyieldingly."

This was the straw that broke the camel's back and Sosabowski spoke again, this time in English, which apparently became more fluent the angrier he got. He told Thomas the crossing was not of sufficient strength to influence the fighting north of the river and would be a needless sacrifice. Horrocks put a stop to it all by stating that the orders given by Thomas would go ahead as planned and if Sosabowski was not prepared to carry them out, a new commander would have to be found. Browning, present throughout, did not say a word. The meeting ended.

However, Browning did take Sosabowski to Nijmegen for lunch at his H.Q. During this time Browning admitted there were very few boats in the Nijmegen area, with the majority being stuck somewhere in the corridor leading to the area. Sosabowski told Browning what he thought of British commanders who carried out a major operation across a series of wide rivers without making sure boats were towards the front. Captain Jan Lorys, one of the staff officers said later, "This was probably the final nail in his coffin, daring to criticize British generals."

The actual crossing by the Dorsets started three hours late at 0100 on Monday 25th September. Initially heavy supporting artillery fire kept the German heads down and most of two rifle companies and a H.Q. element got across. But by 0215 the operation was stopped because the German fire was becoming more intense, although several hours of darkness still remained. Around 300 men from the Dorsets got across and had little impact on the fighting, as predicted by Major-General Sosabowski.

Further east around Driel, at around 2245, a British officer appeared and told the Polish engineer commander Lieutenant Szczygiel that he was to give up his boats. After checking with H.Q. he gave them up. Sosabowski had received a 'request' from 43rd Division to turn its boats over to the Dorsets. So at 2245 the Polish crossing was cancelled, probably to the relief of many a Polish paratrooper.

This ended the attempts to get across the river from south to north.

Final words

So what happened to the P.P.B. after Operation Berlin? Their first move on the morning of the 26th was to Nijmegen on foot, although Major-General Sosabowski went ahead to Browning's H.Q. to receive further orders. He reported their status, advising Browning that he had lost about 400 men, about 23% of the officer strength and 22% of his men. In spite of this weak position, Browning said he knew of the Brigade's difficulties during the battle and intimated that it would eventually return to England but due to the situation it was still needed in the area. The P.P.B. was given the task of defending airfields in the area of Neerloon. With this task came another slap in the face – the Brigade were to be under the commander of 157th Brigade, Brigadier Russell. The men were moved to this area by trucks that evening. After settling in, Sosabowski fired off a letter of protest to Browning. He stated that he felt the P.P.B. was a functioning 'independent' formation and there was no reason that it, and he, a major-general, should be put under the command of a junior officer. This done he then started on a report for General Sosnkowski, the Polish Commander-in-Chief.

Meanwhile, Marek Swiecicki made it across the river and met with Sosabowski who told him that he needed to get back to London as a matter of some urgency to put the Polish side of the battle across. He was back in London in a few days and started work on what was probably the first book published about Arnhem.

The P.P.B. remained in the Nijmegen area and later came under the command of the US 82nd Airborne Division, before being relieved on 7th October 1944, they arrived in England a few days later and were sent on leave.

50 Poles were killed at Oosterbeek or drowned in the evacuation and another 42 were killed south of the river. Worse was to come.

When looking for a scapegoat for the failure of Operation Market Garden, the senior commanders decided to use the P.P.B. On 17th October 1944, Field Marshal Montgomery, the commander of the 21st Army Group, wrote to the Chief of the Imperial General Staff, Field Marshal Sir Alan Brooke that the "P.P.B. fought very badly and the men showed no keenness to fight if it meant risking their own lives. I do not want this brigade here and possibly you may like to send them to join other Poles in Italy."

A month later, Browning write a long letter (the text of which is reproduced as Appendix B) to Lieutenant-General Sir Ronald Weeks, Brooke's deputy, reporting on Sosabowski's command during the recent operation. On 9th

December 1944, Sosabowski was informed by the Polish President-in-Exile, Wladyslaw Raczkiewicz, that he was being removed from his command. The letter gave no reason for his dismissal and even stressed "the merits of your service in this post and your proven character on the battlefield." Browning was on the verge of going to South-East Asia in a new job; in my humble opinion he was the instigator of this shameful act.

Sosabowski handed over command to his deputy, Lieutenant Colonel S. Jacknik; two of the Polish units went on hunger strike at Christmas as a protest, but it all came to naught. The P.P.B. never went to Poland and never reverted to Polish command after its first operation, both of which had been promised. At the end of the war, they acted as part of the occupying forces in Germany, where they stayed for about two years before returning to England in 1947 to be disbanded.

Appendix B

Letter sent to Lieutenant-General Sir Ronald Weeks about Major-General Sosabowski by Lieutenant-General Browning

Personal and Confidential
Headquarters Airborne Corps
APO England
20th November, 1944

Sir,

Report on Major-General St Sosabowski, Commanding 1st Polish Parachute Brigade Group

I have the honour to bring the following facts to your notice with regard to Major-General St Sosabowski, Commanding 1st Polish Parachute Brigade Group, before and during Operation Market.

During the weeks previous to Operation Market, a period which entailed detailed planning for three other possible operations, the 1st Polish Parachute Brigade Group formed part of the force envisaged.

Both during this period, and in fact, ever since the 1st Polish Parachute Brigade Group was mobilised in July, Major-General Sosabowski proved himself to be extremely difficult to work with. The 'difficulty' was apparent not only to Commanders under whom he was planning but also to staff officers of the other airborne formations concerned.

During this period he gave me the very distinct impression that he was raising objections and causing difficulties as he did not feel that his brigade was fully ready for battle. When the brigade was first mobilised I made it absolutely clear to this officer, and in no uncertain terms, that I was the sole judge of the efficiency of his brigade and it was merely his duty to get them ready and train them with all the determination of which he was capable.

It became apparent during this training period that, capable soldier as this officer undoubtedly is, he was unable to adapt himself to the level of a parachute brigade commander, which requires intimate and direct command of his battalions. He left too much to his Chief of Staff and attempted to treat his parachute brigade as if it were a much higher and bigger formation.

During Operation Market the brigade was unfortunate in being dropped in parts owing to the weather. However, during this period of Operation Market great difficulties were being overcome hourly by all formations of the Second Army in their efforts to reach the 1st Airborne Division at Arnhem. This officer proved himself to be quite incapable of appreciating the urgent nature of the operation, and continually showed himself to be both argumentative and loathe to play his full part in the operation unless everything was done for him and his brigade.

Subsequently, when the 1st Airborne Division had been withdrawn, and the Polish Parachute Brigade Group reverted to my command south of the R. Waal, this officer worried both me and my staff (who were at that time fighting a very difficult battle to keep the corridor open from inclusive Nijmegen to Eindhoven) about such things as two or three lorries to supplement his transport. I was forced finally to be extremely curt to this officer, and ordered him to carry out his orders from then on without query or obstruction.

Both Commander 30 Corps and Commander 43 Division will bear out my criticism of this officer throughout the operation.

Major-General Sosabowski has undoubtedly, during the three years in which I have been connected with him, done a very great amount for the 1st Polish Parachute Brigade Group under disappointing circumstances. He was mainly responsible for the whole of the raising, organisation and training of the brigade. However, this good record cannot be allowed to interfere with the present and future efficiency of the brigade.

I am forced, therefore to recommend that General Sosabowski be employed elsewhere, and that a younger, more flexibly minded and cooperative officer be made available to succeed him.

There are, to my knowledge, two possible candidates now serving with the brigade. The first is Lieutenant Colonel S. Jacknik, who is at present Deputy Commander. This officer has had practically no opportunity to display his powers owing to the somewhat overbearing nature of General Sosabowski's personality. The appointment of this officer would, in my opinion, be essentially in the nature of an experiment.

The second candidate is Major M. Tonn, who commands 1 Parachute

Battalion. This officer has trained his battalion well and, in my opinion and in the opinion of the GSO1 Liaison (Airborne) Lieutenant Colonel Stevens, he possesses the requisite drive and administrative ability to fulfil the appointment.

However, this appointment must remain largely a matter for the Polish Army itself to make and it will probably be better in the long run if new blood be brought in.

Finally, I wish to emphasise again that I consider Major-General Sosabowski is a knowledgeable and efficient soldier and up to the average of his rank, but owing to his outlook, temperament and inability to cooperate he should be given a change of employment.

I have the honour to be, Sir,
Your obedient Servant,
(Sgd) F A M Browning
Commander Airborne Corps.

Personal and Confidential

Lieutenant-General Sir Ronald Weeks, K.C.B., C.B.E., D.S.O., M.C., T.D.,
Deputy Chief of the Imperial General Staff,
The War Office,
Whitehall,
SW1.
Copy to: Commander-in-Chief, 21 Army Group, B.L.A.
Original in the National Archives.

Further reading

Cholewczynski, G., *Poles Apart: The Polish Airborne at the Battle of Arnhem* (New York, 1993)

Faulkner-Brown, H., *A Sapper at Arnhem: The Memoirs of Harry Faulkner-Brown* (Renkum, 2006)

Sosabowski, S., *Freely I Served: Story of Polish Parachute Brigade, World War II* (London, 1960, reprinted Nashville TN, 1982)